ETIQUETTE
FOR MODERNS

A Guide for the Executive's Wife

ETIQUETTE FOR MODERNS

A Guide for the Executive's Wife

ELINOR AMES

WALKER AND COMPANY
NEW YORK

Acknowledgements

The author makes grateful acknowledgement to the following:
The Chicago Tribune-New York News Syndicate
Mr. Theodore M. Black
Mrs. D. W. Cowan

Published simultaneously in Canada by George J. McLeod, Limited, Toronto.

Library of Congress Catalog Card Number: 65-15987

Manufactured in the United States of America

Contents

List of Illustrations

Credits

ETIQUETTE FOR MODERNS

A Guide for the Executive's Wife

1

*Etiquette
for Moderns*

MANY PEOPLE TODAY believe that the most significant characteristic of modern etiquette is the growing trend towards informality. Certainly the trend exists (although it may not be permanent), but it would be misleading to suppose that because our present-day manners have become less formal they can be taken less seriously.

The reason for this has to do with the changing role manners play in our lives. In all the stories of the leaders of industry in the nineteenth century—the "robber barons," the scientists, the inventors—we hear very little to suggest that polite behavior had much to do with business or professional success. Certainly we are not led to believe that the wives of Morgan, Carnegie, Belmont or Edison influenced their husbands' careers in any important social or public way, however much they may have contributed privately.

In the early nineteenth century the business world and the social world were at best merely tangential to one another.

In Europe there was a feeling that to be in business or in all but a few of the professions was a distinct social disadvantage. Although democratic America never felt quite so strongly about this, at least a vestige of the sentiment persisted here also.

But the course of the industrial revolution was inexorable. The life of every modern state became increasingly centered on its economy, and by the twentieth century it was no longer possible to pretend that "business" and "society" had little to do with one another.

No doubt all this had an important effect on etiquette, but it also has had an important effect on business. Good manners, which once were exclusively a matter of social graces, have now also become important to one's business or professional career. Even though codes of etiquette have tended to relax and become more informal, the importance of manners has not diminished because relatively more is at stake. Whereas it was once possible to ruin one's social career at a formal dinner party, it is now equally possible to ruin one's professional career at a backyard barbecue.

The most striking feature in this evolution has been the emergence of the wife as a crucial factor in the progress of her husband's career. No longer can the tired businessman count on tottering back to the evening peace of his suburban home and the quiet sympathy of his homemaker wife. All too often he will find her dressed and bejeweled, waiting to go forth and battle beside him at yet another business dinner. Instead of waiting patiently at home to hear what the boss said to her husband, she may hold the key to her husband's success or failure as the result of what she says to the boss's wife.

How and where does she achieve this "business victory?" By socializing, of course. Most corporations nowadays assume that the wives will accompany their husbands on business trips, to business conventions, to business dinners and gatherings of all kinds. As a matter of fact, at most big conventions special events, lunches, fashion shows and other parties are planned especially for the wives while their husbands are at the conferences. And throughout the year there are numerous company, special group and industry-wide dinners that call for the appearance of the wives of the men who attend.

Social status in the realm of big business is fascinating. The young man in the "Administration Pool" or "Executive Training Program" feels a thrill of pride when he is promoted to a job that includes his wife in business-social gatherings. Yet a friend of mine, the mother of three school-age youngsters, phoned me recently to let me know "the good news" that her husband had been made executive vice-president in his company. "And," she added gaily, "this means I won't have to go to all those business parties anymore. In Jack's position, I can be selective and only attend when I think I'll enjoy it."

Possibly the present-day tendency to hold lengthy conferences, to talk shop at mealtime or over cocktails, brought on the acceptance, the actual inclusion, of the executives' wives whenever feasible. Possibly it was simply the practical attitude that, since it could be considered a business expense, the office might as well "pick up the tab" for forty as for twenty and thus include the wives.

The appearance of wives as an important factor in the political scene came with the Roosevelt administration. Eleanor Roosevelt was careful to avoid voicing her opinion on what might be considered official or government business, but she was never one to stay in the background. As First Lady she made *her own* foreground. Her jaunts were supposedly in the interests of "good works," not campaigning. The popular Mrs. John F. Kennedy followed the same pattern. Her role was that of a gracious hostess or a very interesting and attractive guest. Any good will that she built up for her husband was assumed to be incidental. Yet in retrospect, it is difficult to overestimate the political value of the roles played by these two great First Ladies.

When we consider the bitter criticism leveled at Edith Wilson for "meddling" and "censoring" during President Wilson's illness in his last term, when we realize that a generation ago the average citizen's attitude was "We elected *him* president [or governor or senator], so let his wife stay in the background where she belongs," it is apparent that we've come a long way in our views regarding the "place" of the wife in government and business.

President Johnson gave us an extraordinary example of this when, in accepting the resignation of outgoing Commerce Secretary Luther Hodges, he added, "And I want you to know that every step in your march to success has been greatly aided by that wonderful American lady, Martha."

In commenting on the abrupt way in which Hodges himself was treated by the President, the Washington correspondent of the *New York Daily News* said ". . . his feelings were more than assuaged by a tribute to his wife, Martha." Not knowing Luther Hodges, I cannot pretend to form an opinion regarding his feelings, but I suspect that that parting sentence would have sent many a stalwart statesman of "the old school" to the nearest bar to drown his humiliation!

Regardless of personal views, whether or not an individual woman *wants* to be a part of her husband's climb up the business ladder, the facts are plain: the job, without salary or social security, is nevertheless hers. The benefits are the promotions, the appointments, the salary increases that she helps her husband acquire.

Most of all, it is the job of the wives of young men. The "senior wives" (those married to board chairmen, presidents, various senior officials) may jockey for position, may be friendly, apathetic or jealous rivals in their attitude toward each other. Usually, however, when a man reaches these heights, even a disinterested, tactless or caustic wife cannot hurt him professionally. It is the wives of the men "on the way up" who must be careful, be cooperative, acquiescent, pleasant to all, yet not overly friendly toward any of their contemporaries, lest they inadvertently pick the "wrong" or "unpopular" one as a close friend.

The young woman whose husband has just "made the team" must not accentuate her youth if the other women are all much older. She must dress well but conservatively. She cannot have her husband's boss think that she is a frump, but even more certainly she cannot have the boss's wife think she is "an overdressed flirt."

She must be completely conversant with all the basic rules of polite behavior and she must be acutely aware of how they apply to any given social-business situation. In fact, the things this archtypical young woman must know constitute the body of our modern code of etiquette, for it is largely from her experiences and the myriad experiences of her contemporaries that the code has been fashioned. Modern etiquette manuals are not, of course, written solely for her benefit, but in a very real sense, her need is greater than most.

Let us take a look at a few of the things our junior executive's wife must master in order to compete in the arena of business socializing.

Presumably she takes her table manners for granted. But

very little in her regular daily life helps her to maintain her proficiency. Breakfast is a hectic rush to gulp down coffee while getting Jack off to work and the children ready for school. Lunch is a fugitive sandwich nibbled while running the vacuum cleaner or talking on the telephone. And if dinner is not actually served on a tray, it may achieve an equivalent standard of formality thanks to her—and Jack's —sheer end-of-the-day exhaustion. Through the years it is possible for both of them to acquire some weird mannerisms in this way, the least of which is the simple device of supporting their weary frames by planting their elbows firmly on the table top.

The danger here is not so much ignorance, for nearly everyone knows what constitutes good table manners, but the baleful force of bad habit. Our young matron is wise if she plans an occasional "practice session" for herself and her husband, either at home or at a good restaurant.

Another area where the young executive and his wife can run into trouble is in making and acknowledging introductions. The standard rule—present younger to older, less important to more important, gentleman to lady—is sound enough; but if applied insensitively it can offend precisely the people it is most important not to offend. Thus for a junior wife to make too much of a point of deferring to the greater age of some senior company officer's wife is to court disaster.

Anyone who has ever been in the dismal position of unexpectedly having to perform introductions to a person whose name has been recently learned and promptly forgotten probably need not be told of the importance of "getting" and remembering new names—especially if that someone happened to have been the Senior Vice President. Slightly less obvious but nearly as important for the new man and his comrade-in-arms is the need to learn the exact titles of colleagues and to gauge their significance in the pecking order. Even spellings and initials are important. I know of a man in Hollywood who was passed over for a promotion simply because his wife persistently misspelled the Board Chairman's name on her Christmas cards.

Entertaining and being entertained is a vast and vital subject. The "junior wife" must be a good hostess, a considerate guest and a thorough diplomat. She must reciprocate invitations promptly and entertain gracefully, but she must never attempt to dominate the social scene. She should never "talk shop" in any but the most superficial and perfunctory way, but she should carefully listen to and remember every bit of shop talk she hears. She should avoid talking too much about her home, children or suburb, for this is never as interesting to one of her husband's business associates as she supposes it will be. She should be able to talk to a senior executive about any number of interesting but non-booby-trapped subjects and she must never, never be coy with him lest she infuriate his wife and alarm all the other wives. She must avoid taking sides in emotion-charged discussions and refrain from giving gratuitous advice that might be construed as presumption. She and her husband should arrive at corporate functions on time and should not leave before the ranking couple—or, if the junior couple *must* leave first, they should know how to vanish like the Scarlet Pimpernel, with only an unobtrusive word of thanks to host and hostess.

Another point to bear in mind is that manners vary from place to place. Ours is an increasingly mobile society. Corporation executives, government and military officers, and rising young men in nearly all the sciences and professions can expect that they and their families will more than once be moved about the country and, possibly, the world.

Basic manners hold good everywhere, but regional variations with respect to specifics can be troublesome. There are
places, for example, where it is considered normal for dinner
party guests to bring their hostess a small gift. And then
there are places where to do so would be considered un-
necessarily formal and might result in making the other
guests feel uncomfortable. Nearly every place has its little
conventions as to what constitutes appropriate dress (*and*
make-up *and* jewelry) for any given occasion, and these
may be subtly but importantly different in San Diego, Rome,
New York or Scarsdale. The new couple may not always be
expected to know the local conventions beforehand, but they
will be expected to learn them quickly.

We could go on almost indefinitely, multiplying examples
and citing situations. But the point is clear. Manners and
careers *are* deeply involved with each other. A man and his
wife (and even their children) may come under the critical
scrutiny of business or professional associates in almost any
imaginable situation, from a funeral to a company picnic.
Their behavior will be judged and compared, consciously
or unconsciously, with the behavior of similar young families
aspiring to the same kind of advancement. Perfect manners
alone will hardly guarantee promotion, but inattention to
manners, unfortunately, can easily prevent it.

Is this a good thing? Should not etiquette simply be a
means of making social intercourse more pleasant for all
concerned? Must manners, too, become part of the rat race
for success?

In one sense, these are hard questions; in another, they
are irrelevant. Good manners should be and are something
more than just another entry on an *Executive Qualifications
Form* in the Personnel Manager's office. In society at large,
they perform precisely the function for which they were

developed: to help people get along with one another better. The fact that manners have become involved with business does not change the basic reason for having a code of etiquette. As I have said before, it is not so much the nature of manners as the nature of business that has been affected by the interaction between the two.

Nevertheless it can still be argued that, within the context of business, the harsh penalties that can be imposed for social lapses do somewhat distort the essentially human purposes of etiquette. But this is not a peaceful world and never has been. There have always been penalties of one sort or another attached to displays of bad manners. An ideal society would not exact such penalties, but then in an ideal society everyone's manners would, presumably, be ideal.

If the social-business phenomenon has its faults, it also has its compensations. It creates pressures—even if sometimes rather crude ones—to behave well; and as we know, there are all too many people who probably would never achieve a reasonable standard of polite behavior any other way. But even for people with basically good manners, business socializing can confer some unique pleasures. At its nerve-fraying worst, it is nevertheless always marvelously challenging. And at its best it can be positively exhilarating.

2

*Manners
in Public*

ONE OF THE more deplorable modern tendencies in etiquette is the prevalent assumption that manners can, for the most part, be cast aside when one is on the street, in public conveyances, or in other public places. The truth, of course, is that manners apply everywhere. How can we hope to remember the acts of courtesy so necessary at home or at work if we discard them at other times? Manners are not like hats, to be put on or taken off as we please. The truly well-mannered person is *never* ill-mannered. Moreover, the realm of manners-in-public often includes business colleagues and friends as well as total strangers. It is in no sense merely a matter of practicing for "the real thing."

One important principle that should invariably control our conduct on the street is the good American rule of keeping to the right. Too few people observe this rule; most pedestrians weave from one edge of the sidewalk to the other, irresponsibly and unpredictably getting into other people's way all the time. Especially when we are in a hurry we should remember the traffic rule: Overtake people on their left, pass them on the right—and stay on your own side of the road!

A gentleman always walks on the outside when walking with one lady. Tradition says that he should walk on the outside (curb side) no matter how many ladies he is escorting. Now this is a debatable point. The original reason for his walking on the side nearest the curb was to protect her on days when the streets were in poor condition. There were muddy pools in the dirt surface and the gutter was a dumping place for refuse. Consequently the person nearest the gutter was likely to be spattered with dirty water or worse. Since our modern methods of sanitation have removed this practical reason, some men feel that they can better divide their attention if they are between the women they escort. Certainly it is logical. One sees well-bred men following both conventions, so this has become a matter for the individual to decide.

A lady accompanied by two gentlemen always walks in the middle. Under ordinary circumstances she never takes a gentleman's arm when walking on the street. The exceptions are: When the street is slippery or in bad condition, or when walking on a very crowded thoroughfare. A gentleman takes a lady's arm only to help her to enter an automobile or to assist her at the curb.

Very formal persons consider it improper for a man to raise his hat until the lady he recognizes has bowed her recognition of him. People who are well acquainted, however, generally bow simultaneously. A gentleman who is walking with a lady will of course raise his hat to anyone to whom his companion bows. If one of two men walking on the street raises his hat to a passing lady, his companion does likewise—even though he has never seen the lady before. A gentleman always lifts his hat when a lady speaks to him, even if she is a stranger who asks him for directions. If he picks up something which she has dropped, he lifts his hat and asks, "Did you drop this?" or "I think you lost this," hands the dropped article to the lady, and continues on his way. Under such circumstances, the lady should thank him at once.

Although fundamental rules of etiquette seldom vary, certain changes are made for the sake of convenience or common sense. Because our climate is so trying, a man is no longer expected to stand bareheaded while talking to a woman. He should remove his hat when they start to talk and then, if they begin a conversation, put his hat on again. In the same way, while it is best, if possible, to remove the right glove before shaking hands with a lady—still, if a man can't get the glove off at once, it is not necessary to say (as formerly), "Pardon my glove." A gentleman (other than a clergyman or one in naval or military uniform) always offers to carry a lady's package. She is then free to accept or decline as she chooses. In public, as in the home, a lady precedes a gentleman going up or down stairs unless the stairs are slippery or very steep, thus making it necessary for him to assist her. This is a comparatively recent ruling, however, for in our mothers' day a lady would not dream of allowing a man to follow her up a stairway! There still are advocates of this school of manners, so don't think the elderly gentleman who precedes you upstairs is lacking in breeding. Far from it! He's simply following the dictates of chivalry of a past age. It is good manners, too, when a man and a woman must go through a revolving door, for the man to let the woman go first; he steps back and, as she starts, he can push the door or hold it back as he follows. It goes without saying that well-bred men and women avoid loud talking, pushing, walking with arms linked, or anything that would make them conspicuous on the street.

On first thought, it seems almost unnecessary to say that a gentleman never puts his hands in his trousers pockets. Nor does he gesticulate, or emphasize his remark by poking the person near him. No well-bred person would be guilty of these things. But a look around the average subway train or trolley, a casual glance at the person opposite you in a crowded restaurant, will convince you that too much stress cannot be placed on these elementary points of etiquette. Filing one's finger nails, or performing similar personal offices, is one of the most common public offenses. Twenty years ago a lady would not have dreamed of applying powder or make-up anywhere but in the privacy of her own room. Nowadays, it is permissible to use powder puff or lipstick, if you can manage these rites with neatness and dispatch—but a well-bred woman does not comb her hair or adjust lingerie straps in a public place.

A lady precedes her escort when boarding a bus or any public conveyance. He precedes her when leaving. In this way, he is ready to assist her off. Obviously, when leaving a very crowded conveyance, it is impossible to stand on ceremony, and getting off too often becomes a matter of every man for himself. However, when accommodations and time permit, the rule to follow is "lady on first—gentleman off first." It is useless to suggest that a man offer his seat to a woman passenger. It is so seldom done nowadays that the average woman might faint at the courtesy! I think, though, that young people should be taught to relinquish their seats to those who are obviously very elderly, infirm or physically handicapped. (A word of warning, however: a young woman in her twenties should not offer her seat to a mature but apparently capable woman passenger. Many a career woman has been more annoyed than pleased to have a younger woman, by her manner, imply that she is "old.")

Far more important than the suggestion that women or the elderly be offered seats is the simple rule of consideration for the rights of others. In most big cities today, older people want only to be allowed their rights—no pushing, shoving, "horse play" or rowdyism in public conveyances. The teenagers who, entering a subway train, rush for seats, knocking all out of their way, are a constant worry to older passengers.

In most rural communities, simple courtesy and compliance with traffic laws will take care of many automobile etiquette problems. In congested city areas, as in crowded subway cars, it is difficult to follow many of the etiquette rules. However, here again, we can practice the rules of courtesy. The stalled car won't move faster because motorists in the back sound their horns. It is necessary to start when the light turns green, but it is possible also to give those already in the street time to reach the opposite curb. It is fine to know you are "in the right," but there's no sense in courting a smashed car just to prove you "had the right of way!"

A man seated in a parked car does not hold a conversation with a woman acquaintance while she stands on the sidewalk. A brief exchange of greetings is all right but for a conversation he should get out of the car and stand with her. Even in our modern age it is not good manners for a man to remain seated if the woman with whom he is speaking is standing.

The hostess or owner of the car allows her woman guests to enter the car first and gives them their choice of seats. If a member of the family will drive, it is customary to ask a woman guest if she wants to sit in the front seat.

In Europe, a gentleman places the lady on his right in an

automobile. In this country, it is not always feasible to do this. The lady enters a cab first, leaves the seat next to the door for her escort. Thus, in many cases, she is automatically on the left. The cue here is "Use common sense." If it is convenient for the lady to be on the right, fine. If this would mean stumbling over her, awkwardness in entering the cab—forget it.

One old etiquette rule that can and should still be followed is that, when calling for another, a driver *never* remains in the car, sounding his horn to attract the householder's attention. Correctly, and considerately, he gets out of the car and rings the house bell. If parking difficulties make this impossible, he arranges in advance for the one to be picked up to be waiting at the door or in the lobby of his home at a specified time.

On entering a restaurant, a lady follows the head waiter or captain to the table, with her escort a step or two behind. If there is no host of any kind, the gentleman usually goes first to look for an empty table.

It goes without saying that a considerate woman does not order the most expensive item on the menu (unless she is dining with Mr. Moneybags), but neither does she make a point of scanning the menu for the least expensive dish. She does not complain directly to the waiter if her order is not satisfactory. Instead, just as she tells her escort what she wants and he gives the order, so she registers her complaint with him and lets him take it up with the waiter.

Consideration for others rules that those who have finished their meal should not linger at their table if others are waiting to be served.

Whether or not there are checking facilities, a gentleman removes his hat and overcoat before sitting at the table. A lady, on the other hand, keeps her coat on until she is seated.

Then she drops it off her shoulders or slips her arms out of the sleeves. She never checks her coat or wrap unless in a place in which there is dancing. (Obviously, a coat, fur or pocketbook should never be left at a table if all occupants of that table are dancing.)

When a lady at the table leaves or returns to it, all gentlemen in the group rise. So, too, a gentleman rises if a lady stops to talk to anyone at his table. Since he must remain standing as long as she stands there, a considerate woman makes her "visit" brief or sits down at the table so that he may be seated and continue his meal.

Those who are really courteous are as considerate at the theater, opera or a concert as they are in their own home. The first rule is: Arrive on time. Those who push into a row of seats just as the theater is dimmed or the curtain goes up usually disturb most of those they have to pass to get to their seats.

As to entering a theater, if an usher is on duty, the lady follows the usher, preceding her escort. She always enters the row first. He leaves first and turns to help her as she steps into the aisle. In passing others, it is customary to say "I'm sorry"; if they rise to let you pass, "Thank you" is equally correct. Such expressions as "Pardon me" are not best taste. It is correct to face the stage, with back to strangers in the row you must pass through, but, when possible, face those in your own party whom you pass to get to your seat.

A man assists his seated woman companion to slip off her coat, which is then draped on the back of the seat. If she is wearing a hat that may in any way obstruct the view of others, she should remove it. (Women should remember that a very high hairdo or an elaborately dressed wig can block the view just as completely as a hat.)

The first rule of church attendance is "Be on time." If you

arrive late, make your entrance inconspicuous. If possible, wait until the service is finished; if this is out of the question, take a seat in the rear of the church. Rarely is there a "seat offering" in churches today, but if this is paid at the door or if a basket is passed, the gentleman pays for his family or a lady companion. The regular offering, however, is a different matter. Each should give a donation to this, and it is not good form for a woman to have to ask the man of the household for money for the basket. If she must get it from him, the transaction should be an inconspicuous one.

Regardless of the denomination, it is bad manners to laugh or talk in church or to look around, fidget or show disinterest. It is not necessary to actually "take part" in the service if it is not of your religion, but etiquette demands that you outwardly follow the congregation—rise, sit and so on when those around you do.

The advent of automatic elevators has created a few special problems. In an attended elevator in a residential building, gentlemen step aside and permit the ladies to get on first, get off first. The rule has never applied to "business" elevators. In residential elevators, gentlemen remove their hats on entering; not so in business building elevators. In the case of automatic elevators, gentlemen frequently "make a run" to get in the car and either hold the door open or push the "Open" button so that ladies can get in. In most residential and many business cars, one person offers to "push the floors" for all. Since all etiquette rules pertaining to automatic elevators are still in the formative stage, don't bank on this. The sensible thing is to push the button to indicate your floor as soon as you enter the car.

One important rule often overlooked is that we should hold the door open for the one immediately following. If a man and a woman reach a door at the same time, he holds the door and lets her enter first. In a crowded business building lobby, however, this is seldom feasible, and the sensible course is "enter and hold the door for the next one." Thus the man may let the woman enter first, she then holds the door for him. (If someone is holding a door, it is extremely bad manners for others to rush through the open door, ignoring their obligation to put out a hand toward the door in passing through it. So, too, if one going out holds the door to permit another to enter this does not mean he is "frozen" to the door to hold it for all who follow.)

No comments on manners in public would be complete without a reference to careless talking in public places. It is always bad manners to discuss one's private affairs in public. It is equally wrong—to say nothing of being imprudent— to mention names, addresses and so on of friends, business associates or contacts of any kind.

Finally, don't discard envelopes or magazines bearing your own or another's name and address. It doesn't take a minute to tear up your name, and remember, if it falls into the wrong hands it can cause you trouble or, at least, annoyance.

3

Appropriate Attire (What to Wear When)

First impressions are vitally important. All the subsequent judgments we may make about a person will to some extent be conditioned by the very first thing we thought about him. Many a job interview has invisibly collapsed at the moment when the prospective candidate first walked through the Personnel Officer's door. Many a young man's professional hopes have been silently blighted from the moment he first introduced his wife at a company function. And many a young matron's hopes of being invited to join the local Junior League have been stillborn when she unknowingly first met some member of the Admissions Committee at a cocktail party.

First impressions are composed of a number of things—looks, grooming, expression, quality of voice—but paramount among them is the impression created by attire. One may compensate for most defects in appearance, but not for incorrect dress. Obviously you cannot help your pug nose, and no one would seriously consider it a liability, especially if you were plainly a person of charm and taste. But just as obviously you *could* have chosen to wear something other than that flamboyant, too-tight red dress and those bangley earrings at the formal tea given by the Ambassador's conservative wife. That was a mistake for which you alone were responsible, and it may be a long while before you are forgiven.

When I was growing up we were taught that the old-fashioned notion of "Sunday go-to-meeting-clothes" was passe. Youngsters were exhorted to dress neatly and correctly at all times. Above all, we were impressed by the importance of "dressing appropriately." This did not mean "appropriate to one's state in life"; it meant that one should dress suitably for the occasion.

Nowadays a look around will convince even the least clothes-conscious that although it may be impossible to get people to dress "neatly and correctly at all times" we should take a leaf from early American convention and at least "dress up" on Sundays. We must remember that our ancestors had to make many of their own clothes, even spin the cloth from which clothes could be made, yet they knew enough to don their "Sunday best" or brush and press their threadbare garb before starting to church, town meeting, a visit with friends or to view the remains of or the shrine to a national hero. Isn't it appalling, then, to realize that in a better-fed, better-clothed and better-educated society clergymen have to post notices in church vestibules asking parishioners and visitors to wear proper attire, just as restaurateurs have to remind their patrons that unless dressed appropriately they cannot be served!

Fashion and style have nothing to do with "proper" attire. Of course, very old-fashioned or out-moded clothes will make one conspicuous, but the wrong kind of clothes will, in addition to being conspicuous, show you up as either lacking in manners or as appallingly ignorant.

What then is "appropriate" attire? Clothes that "fit" the occasion. Well-cut slacks and a turtleneck sweater are fine for country walks, some sports events, working in your garden, possibly walking the dog. They are not appropriate for church service, an afternoon tea in the city, a pilgrimage to a national shrine (such as the grave of ex-President Kennedy) or for dinner in a smart restaurant. Despite the fact that many "fancy pants suits" are designed and are made in brocades and velvet—even mink and leopard—good taste dictates that these be worn as "at home garb," all the designers and fashion experts notwithstanding! So, too, the sleeveless, be-ruffled black dress that is fine for discotheque or theatre wear is not appropriate in classroom or office.

It is not possible to give specific rules about attire because way of life, finances, place of residence, occupation, activities and general interests all play a part. Also, the truism that times change applies to our wardrobe as well as our conventions. After all, "attire" is based on and important to social conventions. Nowadays many women work outside their homes; most women at some time do some work within their homes. So we find that although some women (men, too) may change clothes before lunch more usually what is donned in the morning will be worn until nearly dinner time.

Having (we hope) relegated pants and shorts to the country or dog walking in town, what is average attire for an average day in the city? A suit, spectator-sports or simple afternoon dress, a dress-and-jacket ensemble, skirt, blouse and/or sweater and skirt, worn with a sport jacket, blazer or sweater, a cloth or fur coat in season.

If a hat is worn, it should "go with" the costume. (A rhinestone-trimmed satin hat is not appropriate with a bulky sweater coat or tweed suit.) A well-dressed woman wears low or mid-low heeled shoes with daytime street clothes. She wears a medium high heel with an afternoon dress. She reserves very high heeled slippers for festive dinner, theater and other after-dark parties, although she may prefer a low or medium heel even on festive occasions.

At present it is impossible to suggest what to wear to the theater, the opera or dinner. Each year fewer and fewer men dress for dinner. (We've reached such an appalling low in "casualness" that a request for a "dress shirt" usually produces a standard white shirt. Most shops designate dress shirts as "evening" or "formal" shirts.) With the decline in dressing for dinner, most men go to the theater or opera (unless it is an opening or Monday night at the "Met") in business or day clothes. If her escort does not dress, a lady should wear a street-length dinner dress or theater suit. Of course theater parties, special benefit groups, attendance at pre-theater dinners mean more dinner jackets for the gentlemen, more floor-length or intermission-length—certainly more elaborate—dresses for the ladies. It is not vital that patrons dress formally, but it is important that they dress neatly and appropriately. This means a neat dress suit or skirt-and-blouse outfit for a woman and a collar and tie and jacket for her escort. This means feminine hairdos should be fixed *before* the performance. Even in "standing room" a performance of the opera is not the place for a head covered with metal clips or huge rollers, whether or not covered with a scarf.

For dinner at home or the average "men won't dress" dinner gathering, simple afternoon dresses or short and conservative dinner or cocktail dresses are usual.

It should not be necessary to tell a sports enthusiast what to wear, other than to admonish him to comply with rules. If only white attire is permitted on the tennis courts, it is bad manners to insist on playing while dressed in brown slacks and yellow shirt. The average golf club allows some leeway in garb, but be sure there are no specific restrictions before going on the course.

Spectators' attire often creates a problem, however. A broad or very high hat can well block the view of those in back at a tennis match. High heels and flamboyant colors are out of place if you're part of the gallery going around with competing golfers. A high hairdo or wig can seriously block the view of others at a theater, movie or sports event.

Remember that finery that is worn should be discarded. The crepe or chiffon dress that is too shabby to wear in public is not appropriate for wear at home. The members of your family are entitled to see an attractive you! Don't wear discards in the house or under a coat when you go shopping.

Here are a few of my favorite "don'ts:"

Don't wear sport gloves with a dress coat and don't wear white kid or pearl or other elaborately trimmed gloves with a sport outfit, such as a tweed suit, flannel jumper and the like.

Don't wear sport shoes, sneakers or moccasins with a dress coat.

Don't wear a sport coat with a dressy dress or hat or a dress coat over shorts and a sweater.

Don't wear an elaborate or low-cut dress to school or office. If you have a social engagement immediately after business hours, wear an afternoon dress or a dress-and-jacket combination.

Don't wear a day-style coat (and certainly not a hat) with a formal evening dress. If you must travel a distance, a short and simple dinner dress is your best choice for wear beneath a regulation coat.

Possibly because there is less variation in men's clothes, there is a tendency to direct most "clothes advice" to women, but men should not be overlooked.

For general day and informal evening wear a business suit, slacks and conservative sport jacket or blazer are usual. A topcoat, raincoat or overcoat and appropriate hat may be added according to the weather. During the summer months all types of tropical wools, cottons and synthetics are usual. May 15 is considered the date for bringing out a straw hat, although some men go hatless all year and many wear a lightweight felt hat in preference to straw.

Formal day wear is seldom worn nowadays, other than for weddings, formal or government-type functions, and state funerals. Six o'clock in the evening is the accepted "change-over" hour. Before six formal wear consists of a morning coat, gray-striped trousers, gray and black or gray, white and black tie or ascot, and a silk (high) hat. For semi-formal wear (most weddings, christenings, many directors' meetings, possibly a formal tea) striped trousers with a single-breasted, braid-edged lapel jacket (walker or stroller) and a derby or conservative homburg or fedora hat is correct. Gray gloves are always worn with semi-formal day attire, and either gray or white pigskin may be worn with formal day clothes.

In the evening (after six o'clock), full dress (white tie and tails) with dress shoes or pumps and an opera (high or collapsible) hat is correct for strictly formal wear. Dinner clothes with a black tie, black homburg, derby or a fedora should be worn for most evening functions, such as

WHAT TO WEAR

OCCASION	WOMEN	MEN
Informal Day		
Office, shop., school, etc.	Suit, dress-jacket combination, simple afternoon dress, spectator sport attire. Avoid overdressing, much jewelry.	Business suit, slacks and sport jacket or blazer.
Formal-Afternoon		
Wedding, christening, lunch, tea, cocktail party, reception, etc.	Afternoon dress, coat, dressmaker suit, fur or furs, non-sport type coat, "dress" hat, gloves, jewelry, perfume.	Dark business suit, white shirt, tie, black shoes. Morning clothes (cutaway with striped trousers, white shirt with plain or pleated bosom, dark or light-gray waistcoat or vest, high hat and gray gloves). A dark oxford stroller jacket may be substituted for morning clothes. With it a homburg or derby.
Semi-Formal		
Evening wear	Simple dance or dinner dress, theater suit, dressy afternoon dress or costume suit. No hat. Evening wrap, furs. Avoid street coat and hat. Long or short gloves.	Dinner jacket with starched or semi-starched plain or pleated shirt (attached collar preferred). Gray or black felt hat.
Formal-Evening		
Balls, formal or state dinners, debutante dances, etc.	Ball gown, formal evening dress, evening coat, wrap or furs. Jewelry, evening slippers and accessories may be as elaborate as desired. Long or medium long gloves. Avoid street coat and hat!	Full dress (white tie and tails) white vest and tie, stiff-bosom shirt with separate wing collar. Dress overcoat, white gloves, high hat, black dress shoes. Links, waistcoat (vest) buttons, etc., should match and be pearl, gold or platinum.
Sunday Wear		
City walking, visiting museums, shrines, attending funeral, memorial or any kind of religious or patriotic service.	Suit, conservative afternoon dress, dress or conservative coat, gloves. Hat if required for religious service. Avoid sweater and pants or shorts outfits, sneakers or other sport shoes.	A conservative business suit or pressed slacks with blazer or sport jacket. Avoid: Sport shirts, sports sweaters, sneakers.

dinners, theater parties, small dances and so on. Full dress is always preferred for balls. (Note: Don't call evening clothes a "dress suit," and remember that although it is often called a "tuxedo" the proper name for semi-formal attire is "dinner jacket" or "dinner clothes.")

Because it is assumed that social life is curtailed in summer, formal clothes (both day and evening) are never worn in the summer months. A lightweight business suit in light or dark tone is correct for day wear in the city, with a lightweight dinner jacket (white, light gray or black) for "dressy" evenings. In the country white flannels and navy blazers may substitute for a summer dinner jacket, although the latter is also correct. Country day wear depends on the community and the occasion. Shorts or slacks and a casual shirt is standard for all informal day wear. A blazer or jacket is added for "dress" occasions, such as a lunch or cocktail party, church attendance, Sunday visiting and so on.

4

Introductions and Greetings

POSSIBLY IN NO other area of etiquette is there such a miasma of doubt as seems to hover over all but the simplest of introductions. For some reason the young man who does not hesitate to take his wife to a fashionable restaurant will panic when he has to introduce her to an older business acquaintance. The hostess who can manage a formal dinner dreads having to introduce the guests. There is really nothing difficult about introductions. There are, of course, a few basic rules, but we should remember that a badly made introduction is preferable to none at all. All too often we avoid introducing people because we are not sure of the form or wording necessary. Sometimes we avoid an introduction because a name escapes us. In this case we should admit and apologize for the memory lapse, ascertain the name and make the necessary introductions.

The basic rules to follow are:

1. The gentleman is presented to the lady unless he is extremely old and she is young, or in the case of a man of importance, a guest of honor, and so on.

2. The younger is introduced to the older.

3. The lower rank is introduced to the higher rank.

Contrary to a too widely held view, the name of the one who "accepts" an introduction is said first, for we are actually asking her permission to introduce another, as "Miss Smith—Mr. Jones." The formal version is "Miss Smith, may I present Mr. Jones," but this is seldom encountered nowadays.

Although young people are sometimes unsure as to which name is mentioned first, most of us have no difficulty with the simple introduction. The real trouble comes when we have to introduce several people. What to do? If Mr. Jones is to be presented to a group, all ladies' names are first, as "Mrs. Brown, Miss Dee, Mrs. Green, Mr. Brown, Mr. Green —Mr. Jones." It is no longer necessary (or chic) to say, "Mrs. Brown—Mr. Jones. Miss Dee—Mr. Jones," and so on.

When several are to be introduced or when two groups meet and most know a few but none know all, a group or "roll call" informal introduction is the solution. In this the "introducer" mentions all ladies, then all gentlemen. This eliminates the long-drawn out, "Mr. Smith, do you know Miss Jones? I think you know Miss Brown," and so on.

Unless there is a great disparity in age, it is never tactful to make a point of presenting the younger to the older (especially when two ladies are to be introduced) since one who is in the thirties does not expect or appreciate deference from someone a scant ten years younger.

Almost as embarrassing as the one who avoids making introductions is the one who makes unnecessary ones. An example is the young executive accompanied by a client who meets a remote business acquaintance in a bus, train, crowded theater lobby or the like. No introduction is expected or made under such circumstances. Obviously an introduction should always be made when people will be together for a time, when there is good reason to believe they may meet again or if they have something in common. This is not the case in a casual encounter or accidental meeting, so an introduction is pointless. It is always permissible to ask "Have you met . . ." However, it is not tactful to ask a lady, in his presence, if she has met a gentleman. This implies that such a meeting would be important to her, whereas chivalry decrees that we take the attitude that *he* is honored by meeting her. So, too, although it is permissible to ask one guest to cross the floor to meet another, we always try to ask the gentleman to meet the lady. At a large party or in any big gathering such as a convention, however, it is sometimes necessary to take the lady to a gentleman, since it might be almost impossible to leave her, go to him, and bring him back for an introduction. In such circumstances, of course, one apologizes to the lady or asks her "Do you mind coming into the other room with me? I'd like to introduce Mr. Smith and he's in there—but there's such a crowd!"

When a husband or wife is introduced to friends, first (given) names are used. A wife says, "Mary, this is Bill," never "This is Mr. Jones" or "My husband, Mr. Jones." If the first name would not be sufficiently clear, she says, "I'd like to introduce my husband, Mary—Bill." A man introduces a business friend as "Jane, this is Bill Jones." Bill Jones correctly says "How do you do, Mrs. Smith."

Your fiance is introduced to family and friends as "Aunt Jane, this is Joe Green" or "Mrs. Doe, this is my fiance, Joe Green." Needless to say, such expressions as "boy friend" are not used, unless jokingly, in polite society. A man is either a fiance or he is "a friend" and no explanation is made. It is bad manners to speak of one who is being introduced to persons other than those in the family as "my friend," since this implies the other person is not a friend.

A young girl or man may be introduced by given name. Older persons are "Mr.," "Mrs.," or "Miss," and we should be a little restrained about adopting the use of first names in this regard. Even though all around you are calling the wife of the Senior Comptroller "Nancy," address her as "Mrs. Jones" until she suggests the first-name basis.

A doctor is introduced socially as "Dr. Jones." A married woman doctor is "Dr. Smith" in professional circles, but socially she and her husband are referred to and introduced as "Dr. and Mrs. Smith" or "Mr. and Mrs. Green." It is perfectly proper to add "Mrs. Green is a doctor," but "Dr. and Dr. Smith," "The Doctors Smith" and "Mr. and Dr. Green" are not correct.

A clergyman, whether Protestant, Catholic or Jewish, who has a degree of Doctor of Divinity is addressed and introduced as "Dr. . . ." If he has no degree, a Catholic or Episcopal clergyman is "Father," a Jewish clergyman is "Rabbi," a Lutheran is usually "Pastor" and most other Protestant faiths are simply "Mr. . . ." Such expressions as "Reverend Smith" and "The Reverend" are not good form. It might be added that, whatever your own religion, you should address a clergyman of any faith in the approved form.

Although a justice or judge is so introduced (socially, too), in this country a lawyer is always introduced and referred to as "Mr. Jones."

Ladies as well as gentlemen are presented to the President of the United States and, regardless of their religious affiliations, to the Pope, a cardinal, a bishop or any other ranking clergyman of any faith. On introduction, a Roman Catholic kisses a Catholic bishop's ring. A Protestant may do so, but most simply accept it as a formal introduction. Most Protestant bishops just shake hands and Catholic bishops are inclined to do this unless in church or religious surroundings.

It is neither necessary nor possible to introduce all the guests at a large party, but the host or hostess should see that a newcomer is introduced to a few people nearby. Actually, it is usual to speak to those around you at a large home party, as your presence is considered a general introduction.

The considerate hostess gives those she introduces a conversational opener in order to break the social ice. For instance, "Mrs. Brown—Mr. Jones" is not much help, but if the hostess adds "I understand you are both New Englanders" or "Jack has just joined the International Division at Union Carbide," there is a ready-made subject for polite small talk.

So much for the one who makes the introduction. What about those who are introduced? The introduction is acknowledged with a simple "How do you do." The gentleman shakes hands when introduced. This is optional with ladies, although at present there is a marked tendency for them to shake hands. Obviously the younger woman or any man waits for the older woman to extend her hand. However, if the one being introduced impulsively puts out a hand, the lady extends hers at once, since being a *lady* she would not cause anyone embarrassment.

I think it is a good idea to repeat the name of one introduced since this fixes it in your mind and adds a gracious, friendly touch. Incidentally, if you don't "get" the name of one being introduced, the time to say so is right then! Too many of us remain unsure whether it is "Mr. Bank" or "Mr.

Blank." This isn't important if you don't meet again, but it can be embarrassing if you continue the acquaintance socially and somewhat worse than embarrassing if you hope to continue it professionally.

There are two errors to avoid in accepting an introduction:

Don't say "We've met before" or "We know each other" if your previous meeting was long ago or a casual one or—and here is where people often err—if you're meeting a public figure or top-level executive who meets many people in the course of a year. Such a person could not be expected to remember you, and a reference to a previous introduction is bound to be embarrassing.

Don't be too quick to use first names. This faux pas can have both business and social repercussions. A new employee is introduced to another older man—"Jack, this is Bill Brown, a new member of our staff," followed by "This is Jack Green, our Treasurer." Obviously young Bill Brown should say, "How do you do, Mr. Green" and wait for the suggestion "Call me Jack." Instead he says, "Hello, Jack" and incurs the dignified Mr. Green's displeasure.

Such expressions as "Pleased to meet you" and "Happy to make your acquaintance" are not good form. You should only say you're glad to meet someone or "This is a pleasure" if you're presented to one who is prominent, a public figure or of whom you obviously could have heard. A word of warning: "I've heard so much about you" is a flattering comment to make to a public figure, a new author and so on, but is embarrassing to anyone else. In fact it is almost as bad as greeting a girl's new beau with "Jane has talked so much about you."

If a hostess makes an introduction and leaves you, don't panic because you can't think of anything to say. It's trite but safe to comment on the weather or the party. If words fail you completely, just remember that the other person shares the conversational responsibility, too, and wait for him to say something.

"How do you do" is the usual greeting; "Hello" is only to be used for your contemporaries. "Hi" (so popular at present) is entirely out of place as a greeting. Young people sometimes skip the salutation and rush right into a conversation with, "Jane, when did you get back?" or "Jack Smith— I thought you were in Europe."

A well-bred man or woman always bows to a passing acquaintance. A man wearing a hat raises it in greeting. He removes his hat when he stops to speak to a lady. (In bad weather she urges him to replace it at once.) In formal circumstances or if they are only slight acquaintances, a gentleman waits for a lady to speak before he speaks to her. In the case of those who are well acquainted, however, this formality is overlooked and the greeting is simultaneous. A man seated in a parked car or on a porch should not call to a girl of his acquaintance and remain seated while they talk. Instead, he should get out of the car or walk down the porch steps and remain standing while he speaks to her.

When shaking hands whether in an introduction or a greeting, it is not necessary to remove the right glove. If the one whose hand you'll take is gloveless and you *can* easily remove your own, you may do so. However, in most cases one who is wearing a glove can't get it off in time. Don't, then, struggle with it or (even worse) mumble "Pardon my glove." It is not necessary or advisable to apologize for the fact you have a glove on. Bear in mind, also, that whenever gloves are a part of formal indoor attire they are not removed when shaking hands.

This chapter would not be complete without a reference

to the indirect introduction—by letter or telephone. A letter of introduction, whether social or business, is always
given unsealed. Years ago the recipient sealed it at once
in the presence of the writer—thus implying his faith in
the other. Nowadays this is seldom done and the letter may
be delivered unsealed by person, and sealed if it is sent
through the mail. One who arrives in a strange city with a
letter usually phones the addressee, introduces himself,
mentions their mutual acquaintance and asks permission to
send the letter. Under such circumstances a gentleman usually suggests a meeting; a lady may agree that the letter be
mailed or may ask the stranger to call and bring the introduction. A business letter of introduction is taken to the office of the one to whom it is addressed and (sealed) may be
given to his secretary to take to him.

5

Conversation

THE ABILITY TO hold an interesting or at least facile conversation is an asset so important in business and social gatherings that it almost transcends the category of etiquette. Usually when a person is judged on his manners the verdict is confined to whether they are good or bad. But when someone is judged on his conversational ability, it is his intelligence that is being assessed. In business socializing particularly this sort of evaluation occurs constantly, and from it senior company officers can draw far-reaching conclusions about the relative qualifications of junior colleagues and their wives. Indeed I know many Personnel Directors who insist that they can tell more about a prospective employee from a desultory chat than from all the *curricula vitae* and personal references in the world.

All this makes the art of polite conversation sound rather formidable. Actually it is not. Good talk is one of the great civilized pleasures and, fortunately, there are a few simple rules and precepts about conversation that go far toward making it as easy and enjoyable as it should be. By applying these rules you will not automatically transform yourself into a brilliant conversationalist and a spellbinding raconteur, but they will help you to hold your own in almost any group and, comfortingly, to avoid the pitfalls that are inevitably present in even the most casual chitchat.

Someone has said that in any group there are those who enjoy talking, those who prefer a listener's role. It is well to remember, though, that it takes two or more to make a conversation. One who answers in monosyllables, who contributes nothing to the talk is a strain. Make an excuse to join another group, say you have to make a phone call—but get away from him. In social groups, we strive to maintain conversation, not monologue, so don't monopolize the talk.

How do you find subjects for conversation? Read the newspapers, listen to radio and TV news reports, and keep yourself aware of what's going on in the community around you, in your husband's business, and in the world. If you don't have the time or inclination for reading books, at least read the book reviews in a newspaper or magazine.

Don't ask personal questions. Don't pry. Don't introduce "ticklish" subjects, such as religion, diets, ailments, politics, age, too personal views. Don't interrupt one who is speaking and don't insist that you can tell the anecdote better.

We should all try to cultivate the art of listening. Most men admire a woman who listens—especially to them. An intelligent listener absorbs the things that make him an intelligent talker.

What to do about direct questions that we consider tactless or infringing on our personal or professional privacy? The questioner, whether overly curious, thoughtless or ignorant, is impolite. Don't try to fight bad manners with discourtesy. Ignore the question and if it is repeated say "I'm sorry, but I'd rather not discuss it" or, perhaps better, pass it off lightly with something like "I'll now invoke the fifth amendment."

Truthfulness and candor have much to recommend them but, in our social contacts, something may be said in favor of the "white lie." I don't know why it is but those who say, "I'm going to be perfectly frank" always say something unkind or belittling. Why can't that statement be followed by a compliment? A "white social lie" is permissible when the truth can't help and might hurt. If a friend asks your opinion about a purchase *before* she makes it, you should give your candid view. If she asks your opinion about something that she can't exchange or alter, an evasive answer or harmless fib is the kind thing. A well-known clergyman is said to have made a practice of smiling kindly at proud parents and saying "Well, this *is* a baby" when he was asked what he thought of an unprepossessing-looking child he was about to baptize. He didn't really express an opinion but the parents were happy in the impression that he had admired the baby.

One who is in the habit of "holding the floor" while he tells not-so-new or oft-repeated stories or jokes may be reminded that his listeners have heard it before. Don't, however, squelch a new acquaintance or usually quiet contemporary with "We all know that story." If there is no one else present and a new acquaintance asks "Have you heard . . . ," the tactful rejoinder is "Tell me about it." A blunt "Yes, I know" or "I read that in the paper yesterday" can be devastating to one who is trying to start a conversation.

The hostess, no matter how big or small the party, may use her judgment about controlling the conversation. She can insist that those who are becoming too intense or too loud drop the subject. She should try to see that newcomers or very reserved guests are drawn into a talking group. Knowing her guests, she is a judge of what is animated conversation and what is pointless argument. (In a group of newspaper, radio or TV personnel or politicians what appears like a heated argument can be merely friendly animated conversation.)

Ideally a hostess should give new acquaintances something to talk about. After an introduction she may add "Jack is from Boston" or "Helen is visiting us for a week." These bits of information are usually enough to break the social ice. Lacking this help, one may fall back on the weather or a not too personal compliment. (It used to be considered bad form to mention either!) Actually a comment on the weather can lead to talk of skiing, golf, tennis or travel. "That's a very pretty hat" and "I like the color of your scarf. What shade of blue is it?" are no longer considered too personal, and after a polite "Thank you" conversation may be easy.

A certain amount of inconsequential small talk is a social asset, but when conversation is more serious, personal or business-oriented a good rule to follow is "Think before you speak."

6

Charm, Social Poise and Personality

As we have seen, conversational ability is partly a matter of manners and partly one of intelligence and personality. The same can be said of charm. Yet charm is a more subtle, more elusive thing. We are not judged harshly if we lack it, but if we have it, it can be a devastating social asset. In most business socializing, charm is a kind of grace note— seldom absolutely necessary, yet always helpful and occasionally decisive.

Charm has been defined as "that which exerts an irresistible power to please and attract." Since most of us want to achieve just this, with one person, a select group or all with whom we come in contact, let's try to define if we can a few of the things that help to make some people charming, while others, with good looks, education and wealth, even though they may be liked, certainly cannot be considered "charming."

The mere possession of wealth doesn't give charm, just as

it won't buy happiness (although a teenager recently remarked that "money won't buy happiness, but it will buy
the convertible in which you can go around and look for
happiness!"). It is also possible to be a "lady" or "gentleman" in the accepted sense of these words and still be short
of charm.

Since the meaning of "lady" and "gentleman" changes in
minor ways through the years and because the words recur
throughout this book, I'll define them as I understand them.

According to the dictionary, ladies and gentlemen are
persons of good birth and breeding. Thus they have an
initial advantage over those less fortunately born. Although
we obviously expect more of them, this does not mean that
one born to humble circumstances cannot have better "natural" manners. The truly gentle person not only *acts* kind but
feels kindly toward others. He is never loud, never boastful,
never "pushy." If wealthy, he does not make an ostentatious
display of riches. If poor, he refrains from useless lamenta-
tions about his lot in life, abject apologies for his home, or a
spoken or implied irritation with his parents' lack of polish.

It is well to remember that charm can be natural or acquired but it cannot be learned by rote. When it is natural,
the possessor seems always to do or say the right, the kindly
thing by instinct. There are six requisites for which to strive
in acquiring charm. They are:

Charm of Appearance: Good grooming, neat and appropriate attire, avoidance of careless habits in dress and pos-
ture.

Charm of Manner: One who is charming is kind, does not
gossip, belittle or thoughtlessly condemn another. Consideration for others is possible regardless of one's station in
life.

Conversational Charm: One who is charming is well informed, keeps abreast of the news, is capable of holding a serious conversation or, if circumstances indicate, of indulging in light small talk. This does not mean an attempt to dominate a conversation or to be overly witty. On the contrary, a sense of humor is necessary, but wit if it is caustic can be unkind.

Vocal Charm: It is not possible to be really charming without a pleasing voice. One who possesses charm has trained herself to speak clearly and distinctly and to enunciate properly. It is easy to fall into careless habits of speech so we must train ourselves to occasionally censor our way of speaking, our grammar and pronunciation.

Physical Grace: One who is charming knows how to sit, stand and walk correctly. She knows how to enter a conveyance and cross a ballroom floor.

Concern for Others: Although listed last, this might be listed first in importance. It is not possible to be charming if one is selfish, self-centered or uninterested in another's welfare. The charming woman is quick to put others at their ease; she considers her family's interests as important as her own. She may not be overly friendly toward neighbors, but she is always courteous.

For some reason we are too often inclined to think of charm as a feminine virtue. Obviously a charming woman is a feminine one. But men may be charming in the true sense of the word—in short, charming and manly.

Charm is an accumulation of habits and gestures and points of view. It is good manners and smartness and savoir-faire. Its presence is difficult to define, but its absence is quickly noted.

Poise is defined as balance. Social poise is social balance. We won't have social balance unless we are sure of ourselves. One way to acquire self-assurance is to know social customs, to have a knowledge of etiquette. If you don't know how to accept an introduction, don't know how to eat certain foods, don't know how to address a VIP, you won't be self-assured, hence you'll lack social balance. In trying to build up our personality, our social poise, we should read books and articles on etiquette, make a point of seeing how the table is set in a smart restaurant, which forks are used for given courses, and so on.

Having gained a knowledge of etiquette, make it work for you—not the reverse. Learn which rules may be broken, which may not. Train yourself to differentiate between the essentials and the nonessentials of etiquette and social usage. Above all, keep your sense of humor and avoid extremes. Etiquette is a "ticket" to gain you acceptance. It is not meant to be used as a crutch.

It is well to remember that popularity is a rather nebulous thing. Although it is partly dependent on one's personality, it is also involved with surroundings. The girl who is a good tennis player may be the center of attention in her tennis-minded suburb but will find herself lost in the crowd when all around her at a New York cocktail party are animatedly discussing the new Broadway theatrical season. The man who is popular with his professional colleagues may not fare so well in a mixed group—especially if he can't dance, has no interest in popular music, and has never learned to play bridge or other "social" card games.

Popularity is seldom successfully acquired by directly seeking it, but the person who has an attractive personality and is at ease in most social contacts can, all things being equal, achieve a satisfying degree of it.

Too many people who want to be popular make the mistake of imitating someone else. How wrong they are! The first rule for lasting social success is "Be yourself." Don't

think "I'm plain. I can't attract friends, but if I act like Jane or Helen or some famous actress I'll attain the popularity that comes so easily to them." Realize that you are *not* Jane or Helen or the well-known actress and that, although imitation may be the sincerest form of flattery, it is not the way to improve your personality. If you are naturally quiet, don't try to be the life of the party but do try to contribute something to the group conversation and to make your silence a form of interested listening rather than uninterested wool-gathering. If you don't enjoy the opera, don't try to pretend interest, but on the other hand don't talk and laugh while opera-lovers are listening to favorite recordings.

Most of us are inclined to think that shyness, awkwardness and overwhelming self-consciousness are a sign of great humility. Actually they indicate self-centeredness. One who is self-centered enters a room worrying about the impression she will make, what others will think of her, and so on. The best cure for this kind of awkwardness is to remember the words of a great dance teacher: "Don't worry that everyone will notice you are not a good dancer. Most people are too busy with their *own* dancing." There's one thing to remember, though: If you're really shy and dread attracting attention to yourself, dress conservatively and appropriately and avoid extremes of conduct. Too often the young man who is self-conscious tries to cover it up with too much self-assertion which brings him to the unpleasant notice of others. The timid girl who wears too much jewelry or a plunging neckline doesn't gain self-confidence, nor does she gain admiring glances. She's stared at and thus becomes more ill at ease.

In improving one's personality, the habit of intelligent listening is very important. It has been said that a girl can keep up a conversation with the average man by merely saying "Wonderful," "Do go on" and "You did!" occasionally. I sincerely doubt this. I am convinced that in most cases the young woman has to start the conversation going and then let the man do his share of talking. Too often we don't give men half a chance to talk in social surroundings.

Charm and social poise are not really impossible to attain. We make an effort, and after a while we realize that we have peace of mind and don't seem to make stupid social blunders. Possessing charm, we can agree with Sir James Barrie: "If you have it, you don't need to have anything else."

7

Table Manners

TABLE MANNERS ARE of great importance in business as well as in social life. I'm sure many a salesman has lost an order because his lunch table manners were atrocious. Certainly more than one girl has lost a beau because her manners at dinner did not live up to his first impression of her. Yet to a great extent table manners are based on simple common sense. In most cases the natural way is the right way. If you are not sure which fork to use, see which one the hostess or another guest has picked up. If, as sometimes happens in a restaurant, you are the only one who ordered a certain dish, do what seems easiest and most graceful. If you do make a blunder and pick up the wrong fork, don't be overwhelmed. Ignore your blunder and the chances are that it will not be noticed.

At a home dinner the silver is put down in the order in which it will be used, working in toward the plate. Thus if soup is the first course a soup spoon will be to the extreme right of the plate. Spoons and knives are to the right of the plate; forks, with the exception of a cocktail or oyster fork, are on the left. (If the first course is oysters, the small fork will be on the extreme right.)

Since the fork is considered the more pleasing of the two, whenever possible use a fork instead of a spoon. Put only one kind of food on it at a time, don't use it as if it were a spear.

Although the knife's major use is cutting, it may also be used for spreading butter on bread or rolls. On the other hand, the fork is used for buttering vegetables, putting butter in baked potato, or spreading most types of cheese.

When using a spoon, sip soup and other liquids from the side. One does not put the spoon front first into the mouth. It is permissible to turn the spoonful of cereal or dessert slightly toward the front but save the straight ahead "shovel" technique for spoon-feeding the baby and taking medicine. Drink tea, coffee and other beverages from a cup, using the spoon only for stirring or to taste for temperature or sweetness.

Never introduce unpleasant topics at mealtime. Don't talk about foods, your diet, your ailments. Above all, don't comment about the caloric value or the cholesterol content of the food you are eating! Table conversation should be light, even at family meals. (This means you should avoid constant scolding of the children, and don't bring up the subject of household bills.)

Gentlemen draw back chairs for ladies near them. They remain standing until all ladies are seated. Ladies at the table do not sit down until the hostess is seated.

It is impossible to give definite figures as to the distance of one's chair from the table, for this will depend on the type of chair, your personal preference, comfort and so on.

It is not good manners to sit too close to the edge of the table, but it is equally wrong (and can cause spilled food) to go to the other extreme.

As soon as you sit down, take up your napkin and put it in your lap. When leaving the table, put the napkin at the left of your plate—folded if it is an average home and you will have another meal in the household, slightly crushed (unfolded, of course) if you are a guest for just that meal or in a hotel or restaurant.

The knife and fork should be held firmly but not forcefully gripped. Both the American and European methods of cutting and eating meat are considered correct in this country. In the American—sometimes called "zigzag"—method, the knife is put down on the right edge of the plate and the fork transferred from the left to the right hand to eat the just-cut meat. The European way is becoming increasingly popular, especially along the Eastern seaboard. This consists of cutting the meat, continuing to hold the knife in the right hand while the meat is eaten with the fork in the left hand. In this case, the true European method is to hold the fork "spear fashion," although it may be turned in the hand and held "spoon fashion" as in the American method.

In this country, the knife and fork are never propped on each side of the plate, like oars. They are not crossed on the plate when the course is finished. When not in use or when finished, the silverware is placed on the upper right section of the plate. It is not considered "bad form" (as it formerly was) to "clean" one's plate. This does not mean that every pea, every bit of spinach must be eaten, nor does it mean that gravy may be "wiped up" with a bit of bread. On the other hand, it *is* bad form to leave the food untouched or to refuse each food as it is proffered. The courteous thing is to take a small portion of the food you don't want or cannot eat and, once on your plate, dab it with your fork so that it does not look untouched.

Don't hunch over your plate, don't bend down to your fork; carry the fork up to your mouth, don't rest your arm flat on the table as though guarding your plate. Between courses, sit quietly. Don't play with the silverware or, with your fingers, drum on the table.

In a private home it is impolite to smoke at the table unless the hostess has placed cigarets (or at least ash trays) on the table as an indication that smoking is permitted. If there are no ash trays on the table, assume your hostess does not want you to smoke and don't light up or ask if you may smoke. In a restaurant or other public dining room, you may smoke at any time—even during the meal. Ask your tablemate's permission before doing so, however.

There are times when something must be removed from your mouth. The rule is "Do it as inconspicuously as possible." Please, please don't transfer such bits to the plate with your fork or spoon. Do not screen this process with your napkin! Olive pits, cherry stones and fish, chicken and terrapin bones should be "cleaned" as well as possible in the mouth, before removing with thumb and forefinger. These and any foreign bits taken from the mouth should be placed on the edge of whatever plate or dish will be first removed. Thus, in a choice between putting the chicken bone that was in your soup on the bread and butter plate or on the plate beneath your soup plate or consomme cup, put it on the latter. This will be removed at the end of the course, whereas the bread and butter plate will remain there through the main course.

A lady should not put her purse, gloves, opera glasses or other accessories on the table. Ideally, such articles should be kept in the lap. A package or outsize pocketbook should be put on the floor or the waiter may be asked to bring an extra chair for such belongings.

Food that is served by a waitress or butler is offered at the left. Help yourself without touching the platter or serving dish. For vegetables such as mashed potatoes, peas, spinach and so on it is customary to use only the serving spoon, held in the right hand. Both a serving spoon and fork are usually on the serving dish. They may both be used if you wish. They are both used for meat, fish, chicken-on-toast, string beans or other "stringy" or not compact vegetables. When both fork and spoon are used for service, hold the food between the two in transferring it to your plate.

The serving spoon that is used for gravy, salad dressing or anything served in a bowl or gravy boat should be put back in it, not laid on the serving plate beneath.

For the uninitiated, the awkward or puzzling point in a semi-formal meal often comes when a finger bowl on a dessert plate is put before him. Actually this is simple. The finger bowl and doily beneath should be picked up and placed above and to the left of the dessert plate. The dessert fork and spoon should then be placed on either side of the dessert plate. (When, as is usual, both a fork and spoon are served with dessert, you may use either or both.)

After dessert, dip your finger tips in the water in the finger bowl and dry them on your napkin. This should be done as neatly and quickly as possible. Although it is equally correct to dip the fingers of one hand at a time or both together, the latter is, at present, the more usual and less conspicuous method.

In a maidless home, food is passed around the table toward the right and each guest takes the platter or dish in his left hand and serves himself with his right. If the dish is heavy or very warm, it may be put down on the table for self-serving, then picked up and passed to the next person. (It is never good form to slide a platter or dish along the table.)

Unfortunately, accidents will happen. If there is a maid available and you drop a piece of silver or your napkin, don't pick it up. Ask the maid for another. In a maidless home or if there is danger of someone tripping over the fallen object, retrieve it and place it on the table's edge. Don't use anything that falls on the floor. If you upset a glass, spill food on another or break something at the table, apologize, do what you can to repair the damage without disrupting the meal and later pay (or offer to do so) for the repair, cleaning or what must be done. Don't, *please,* make too profuse apologies, don't continue to talk of your stupidity, your awkwardness, the damage. Under such circumstances, a well-bred hostess smiles sweetly and acts unconcerned. (She can't ruin her dinner party by saying what she thinks of you!)

Here is an outline of the more ordinary foods and the accepted way of eating them:

Finger Foods: Raw apples, raw celery, grapes, bread, candy, crackers, cookies, nuts, olives, radishes, cherries, raw pears, most canapes, potato chips, all but the heart of an artichoke, plain dry cake, "dry" bacon strips and hard-boiled egg slices when served as canapes. Chicken and chop bones are not picked up in the fingers at any but a picnic or snack-type meal. It is, of course, correct to hold the lobster on the plate with the fingers of one hand while removing the lobster meat with the fork held in the other hand. At buffet suppers and cocktail parties, sliced turkey, ham or other meats should not be picked up in the fingers!

Fork Foods: Fish, meat, salad, most vegetables other than artichoke, watermelon, pie, "firm"-type pudding, all moist or fancy cake, club sandwiches, french toast, appetizers served at the beginning of a meal, eggs, other than boiled.

Spoon Foods: Any foods that cannot be gracefully eaten with a fork or the fingers require a spoon. These include applesauce, custard, soft puddings, cereals and obviously soups—even very thick, creamy ones.

Asparagus is usually broken and eaten with the fork, unless it has no sauce or butter on it and is hard and firm enough to be picked up in the fingers. (In most sections of Europe this is considered a "finger" food.)

Artichokes: Pull off a leaf at a time, dip the edible end in the sauce, and bite it off. The hard thistle-like center is scraped away and then the heart is eaten with the fork.

Bread: A whole slice is never buttered at once—unless in making sandwiches. At the table, break off and butter a small piece as you are about to eat it.

Fish: In serving lemon with fish, a quarter wedge is better for squeezing than a slice. The lemon section is squeezed between the thumb and forefinger. Since the object is to get the juice on the fish, hold the piece of lemon near the plate.

Olives, Raw Celery and Pickles are always picked up with the fingers unless they are in a relish or salad. Never dip the celery stalk into the salt dish; shake the salt on it.

Oyster Cocktail: With the oyster fork, take the oyster from the shell and dip it in the sauce.

Salads should be eaten with the fork and, when possible, cut with it. If a hard, cabbage-like lettuce is served, it may be cut with the knife, then eaten with the fork.

Sandwiches: A club sandwich, unless very dry and compact, should be eaten with the fork; the same applies to open-faced sandwiches or any that are moist or from which dressing might drip. Plain sandwiches of all kinds may be picked up in the fingers.

Sherbet is eaten with a spoon when served as dessert, with a fork when served with meat. After eating anything served in a sherbet glass, leave the spoon on the plate beneath. When dessert is served in a low dish or cup with a plate beneath, the spoon is left in the dish itself, not on the plate.

Soup: The soup spoon is turned away from you as you fill it (never more than three-quarters full) so that any that drips will fall in the plate, not on the table or your lap. When finished, the spoon is left in the soup plate, not on the plate beneath. Clear consomme and most light lunch soups are served in bouillon cups or, lacking these, standard size tea cups. The soup is sipped from the spoon. When cool it may be drunk from the cup. The bouillon spoon is placed on the saucer, not in the cup, when not in use. Crackers are eaten with soup, but may only be broken up into it at picnics or other very informal meals.

Don't drink with the spoon in the cup. Don't leave the spoon in the cup when you finish the beverage.

At family or informal meals it is permissible to slightly tip the soup plate *away* from you in order to get more, but don't struggle to get the last drop and *never* tip the soup plate at a formal meal.

Do not talk when you have food in your mouth and *do* keep your lips closed while chewing.

8

Wines, Cocktails
and Liqueurs

THIS YEAR THE average Italian will consume approximately forty gallons of wine. The average Frenchman will consume about thirty-five gallons. Yet the average American will probably consume less than one.

Until quite recently Americans as a people have been remarkably leery of wine-drinking. It is difficult to explain this on the grounds either of the high prices of imported wines (the majority of them have always been less expensive than hard liquor) or the inferiority of domestic wines (many of them are excellent). The real reason, I suspect, is that many Americans have been afraid of showing their ignorance of wines in public. Connoisseurs have made such a point of ranking growths, comparing vintage years, forbidding the service of certain wines with certain foods, insisting on the use of certain types of glasses, and so on and on, that the inexpert have been dismayed and have turned to cocktails and after-dinner drinks for refuge.

This, of course, is foolishness. The average French or Italian wine consumer is no connoisseur. He drinks wine with his meals because it is a pleasant thing to do, and he doesn't know and couldn't care less whether Château Mouton-Rothschild should be rated as *Premier Cru* or *Deuxième Cru.* In fact, he knows very little about wine. But the little he does know provides him with an accurate guide to the enjoyment of this gracious beverage.

There is no reason on earth why any reasonably intelligent adult American cannot learn in half an hour all that the average Frenchman knows about wine-drinking. And there are some very good reasons—apart from the pleasures vouchsafed thereby—for doing so. For if wine is not yet a commonplace adjunct to our everyday meals, it is nevertheless becoming an increasingly familiar element in our entertaining. Any hostess, by making the trivial effort required to learn the basic rules, can grace her dinner parties with that extra touch of elegance that only the service of the right wine can bring. With hardly greater effort any executive entertaining an out-of-town client in a fashionable restaurant can, if called upon, face the wine steward with serene self-confidence.

The easiest way to learn about wines is to read about them in one of the many excellent and entertainingly written books that you will find no farther away than your nearest bookstore or library. After a session with Mr. Lichine, Mr. Churchill, Mr. Simon, Mr. Schoonmaker or any of several other expert mentors in the field, you will probably both know far more about wines than you absolutely have to and not be the least bit sorry for it. Meanwhile, however, let us quickly survey some of the essentials that everyone should bear in mind about wine-drinking.

First, glasses. It is not necessary to have expensive glasses, but they should be stemmed and shining. Although clear glass (crystal if finances permit) is the usual choice, one occasionally sees Rhine wine served in a green glass, and Burgundy and other still red wines may be served in ruby-colored glasses. However, nowadays only old and very elaborate restaurants and hotels, and homemakers who have inherited family glassware, are likely to have colored glasses. (In smart New York society in the early nineteen-hundreds it was considered poor taste to use colored glasses. Good food and drink was of great interest to those who could afford luxuries, and they felt that a red glass was used to conceal the cloudiness of a poor-quality Burgundy.) Actually, even a still red wine has highlights and beauty in a sparkling crystal glass. Ornate or very unusual glasses are "conversation pieces," but a wine connoisseur feels that "a good wine can stand alone" and an overly decorated glass detracts from its contents.

Of course it is not necessary for the average hostess to have a complete stock of glasses. The essentials are water goblets and three-ounce wine glasses. With these she'll just get by. In building up a stock of glassware, the next thought should be for liqueur glasses, then champagne glasses. Claret glasses (smaller than the standard wine glass), brandy snifters and hollow-stemmed champagne glasses are nice to have but far from essential. Ideally all glasses used at dinner should be of the same pattern. However, with the trend toward "footed" rather than "stemmed" water goblets, a compromise is often in order. The stemmed wine glass used with a footed goblet must go with it in general shape and style. If two wine glasses are put at each place at dinner, they should match. A wine and a champagne glass need not be identical but, here again, they must "go" together. In the

FRENCH WINE GLASSES

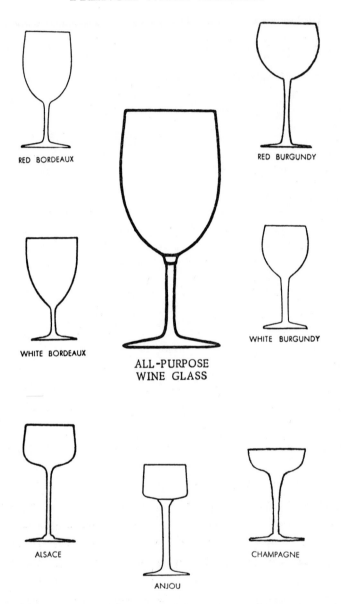

RED BORDEAUX

RED BURGUNDY

WHITE BORDEAUX

ALL-PURPOSE
WINE GLASS

WHITE BURGUNDY

ALSACE

ANJOU

CHAMPAGNE

The all-purpose glass is best for any single wine. When serving more than one, use the appropriate special types. Note: Rhines and Moselles would be served in the Alsatian glass.

last analysis the kinds and number of glasses an individual hostess should have must depend on the size of her family, her budget and how frequently she entertains.

The average homemaker cannot and should not attempt to compete with a wine steward in hotel or restaurant. There are, however, a couple of points for the prospective hostess to remember. Be sure to serve a wine at the proper temperature. Many good wines lose their bouquet if opened in a temperature that does not benefit them. Red wines should be served at room temperature, white wines should be cool, champagne and white Alsatian wine should be thoroughly chilled or, as a wine steward would say it, "well iced." Sherry and Dubonnet may be served at room temperature or chilled, as taste dictates.

The service of a wine is always important. Never purchase a wine a few minutes before a dinner party. Red wine in particular should not be shaken or unsettled when poured. The sediment in a very old red wine should not be shaken up from the bottom of the bottle.

All good restaurants and hostesses who entertain fairly extensively bring red wine to the table in a "cradle," or basket of silver, wicker or chromium. In this the bottle rests on its side. To serve, the metal cap should be removed, the bottle neck wiped clean, then the cork drawn. After decorking and wiping the lip of the bottle, the wine is poured slowly. In public, wine is poured first into a gentleman's glass so that any sediment that has risen to the top will not be in a lady's service. At a home dinner, if a waitress serves, she may pour the hostess' wine first out of consideration for guests. At a semi-formal maidless meal, the host usually decorks the bottle. In this case he pours a little into his own glass first, then fills the glass for the lady on his right, and so on. (If the cork crumbles or breaks in decorking, the wine should be decantered at once.)

Although one still sees sherry served with the soup occasionally—and the practice is not as frowned on in England as it is in the United States—it remains a moot point. Many hostesses insist that this deadens the appetite and spoils the flavor of the wine that follows. Others insist that sherry or Madeira enhances the soup and even claim that the soup itself should be flavored with the wine that accompanies it.

A dry white wine, Chablis, Pouilly Fuisse or a Rhine is appropriate with oysters.

Rhine and Moselle are popular with the fish course although any white wine is correct. White wines are also served with cold cuts, such as ham or tongue, but a roast or other heavy main course calls for a rich red wine.

Wine is never served with the salad course, since we don't mix wine and vinegar. However, if lemon juice or other substitute is served instead of vinegar, the main-course wine may be left on the table during the salad serving.

Despite the popular notion that only champagne may be served with dessert, a sauterne is also correct. Don't, however, serve sauterne with a dessert made with milk or eggs.

Champagne remains the favorite dessert wine and is the luxury favorite also when one wine is served throughout the meal. However, in this case, I suggest a dry champagne *(brut)* with the main meal and a sweeter one *(sec* or *demi-sec)* with the dessert.

When only one wine is served throughout the meal it is brought to the table with the meat course. Either white or red Bordeaux is a usual choice, but we no longer hold rigidly to the ruling "White wine with fish or fowl, red with red meat."

In restaurants, where people in the same party may have chosen a variety of main courses, a rosé is often the wine selected as a compromise. Rosés are pink wines, somewhere between reds and whites in character, and served lightly chilled. If your family has found a wine, either white or red, that all enjoy, serve it throughout the one-wine meal without comment—whether it is a standard domestic, a modest import or a rare vintage worthy of a sybarite.

Cocktails are an American contribution to before-meal drinking. They are supposed to sharpen the appetite for the meal to follow. For the average dinner guest, two cocktails should be the limit.

In a restaurant or hotel, it is usual for the waiter to offer the cocktail list before bringing the menu. In a less elaborate restaurant, a cocktail list is usually at the top of the menu. At a home dinner, of course, the cocktails are served with canapes or hors d'oeuvres in the living room.

It is not unusual to order "fancy" cocktails in a restaurant, but the dinner hostess wisely offers a choice of one or two standards, such as manhattans, martinis or old-fashioneds, and also has Scotch, sherry or Dubonnet, and tomato juice for those who don't like cocktails.

The wise hostess refrains from serving heavy or very filling canapes before dinner. The usual ones are potato chips, nuts, tiny crackers or toast rounds with cheese, minced meat, chopped egg, anchovy paste and caviar. Hot hors d'oeuvres are fine for cocktail parties or the now-so-popular combination cocktail party–buffet supper. They are usually considered "heavy" as a preface to a seated dinner. Among favorite hors d'oeuvres are grilled sausages, tiny meat balls, small patty shells filled with creamed chicken, tuna, minced sardine or other delicacy. In addition to the varieties listed here, carrot sticks, celery, olives and tiny chunks of spiced melon are favorites.

A dinner guest never takes his prefatory cocktail to the dining room table unless the hostess asks him to do so since most of the guests have finished their drinks. He never takes a canape with him or hastily gulps a final one as he starts in to dinner, since this implies a doubt about the forthcoming meal.

Although it is perfectly correct to invite guests for cocktails and assume that they'll go on someplace for dinner, it too seldom works that way. At least some of those invited for cocktails have no evening engagements and the tendency is to linger on long past a normal dinner hour. Even the hostess who has not planned a buffet meal always has coffee, sandwiches, possibly cold cuts for these late-stayers. Sufficient food and coffee can often make the difference between an embarrassingly convivial guest or two and a few who, while they *do* stay, are still pleasant visitors. But if a hostess is going to have these few for an improvised meal, why not plan something a little more definite and let the invitations be for more than "cocktails"? For this reason I find it far more sensible to invite guests to a cocktail and buffet dinner party. The guests who have a dinner engagement won't hesitate to say they can't wait for the buffet; the others follow the cocktails with a simple but substantial supper, at which I always serve at least one hot dish.

Few hostesses nowadays follow the old-fashioned custom of serving the gentlemen's liqueur in the dining room. The modern way is to serve liqueurs with the demitasse in the living room. Although sweet after-dinner drinks are served, cognac, B and B, and other brandy-base liqueurs are also popular. Although such drinks may be served in the standard pony, a balloon glass should really be used for cognac, since this allows for inhaling the rich aroma as well as sipping the drink.

9

*Buffet and
Other Informal Meals*

BUFFET ENTERTAINMENT HAS become an accepted way of life in most sections of the country. Once upon a time no hostess would have dreamed of inviting anyone whom, for business or social reasons, she really wanted to impress to a buffet supper. Now young lawyers and their wives think nothing of entertaining senior partners in this way.

Possibly this is because of the acute shortage of domestic help, but I'm inclined to think our trend toward casualness is also a major contributing force. Whatever the reason, the buffet meal, whether a Sunday breakfast or a complete dinner, has a great deal to recommend it. It allows the hostess in the average home to prepare most of the food in advance. Even if she has a maid, she can't possibly have a seated and properly served dinner for more than six in all. With a larger number, if the maid must go around the table, serving each in turn, the food is bound to be cooled by the time all are served.

This form of entertaining, always popular for breakfasts in English great houses, got off to a bad start in the United States. When buffet suppers were an adjunct to big cocktail parties, when the hostess never thought of allotting table space for guests, a buffet meal often meant that a harassed guest tried to balance a plate on his lap, put his glass or cup and saucer on the floor next his chair, or (even worse) faced the dismal prospect of trying to eat while standing in a crowded room. When we consider that in that era most buffet suppers consisted of cold cuts, baked beans or potato salad, we realize why the guests who came for cocktails usually tried to avoid the buffet.

Today there are three forms of buffet suppers. The usual (and this, like those that follow, may be actually a "dinner" or truly a late evening "supper") features a complete buffet set on sideboard (as the name implies) or on a dining room or refectory table. This consists of plates, silverware, napkins, plates or warming baskets of rolls, bread or muffins, at least two kinds of cold sliced meat, at least two dishes of hot vegetables, one hot meat dish, a salad bowl, relishes, coffee service and cups and saucers. Sometimes the coffee and cups are on a separate table or counter, but all foods and beverages for the main course are in the same general area of the room. The guests help themselves, then find seats at small tables that have been set up in living and dining rooms. If the group is small, a few occasional tables may be sufficient. Possibly the hostess will have recourse to small folding tables especially designed for buffet dining. The point to remember here is that there must be sufficient table space so that guests may eat in comfort.

The buffet service that is rapidly gaining popularity, even among those who have several maids or who engage caterers, is really a semi-buffet and is actually a standard and complete dinner. In this service the dinner table or a series of four-seater tables should be set with silverware, napkins, water and wine glasses, possibly a first course of fruit or shrimp cocktail. In a convenient location a buffet is set up. On it are the heated dinner plates, a roast and its accompanying vegetables, potatoes, hot rolls. Guests either take places at the table or (more usual) look for their place card. Although guests may go back to the buffet for a second helping (and many do), the service thereafter is handled by a waitress. She brings in salad, fills glasses and later clears the table and serves the dessert. Coffee and liqueurs are later served in the living room. This type of service is especially popular with men, who feel free to take what they want and have the comfort of a regular table and chair; and, since this is quicker than the dinner served entirely by a maid, the main course is hot when the guests start to eat.

The third type of buffet is actually a late and light supper. Since only sandwiches, sliced meat and possibly a salad are served with coffee, it may be set up on the buffet or, for a small gathering, the plates of food may be passed by the hostess. This very informal service is sometimes a solution for the young hostess whose space and furniture is limited. It has a disadvantage, however, in that it means putting an assortment of small sandwiches, possibly a portion of salad or sliced meats on each plate. Since many guests won't eat much, this means an amount of waste.

Late suppers fall into two categories—those that are planned and those that are impromptu, almost like "raiding the refrigerator." The former has already been described. The latter depends for its success on the personality of the host or hostess. One who suggests "All come over to my house and have something to eat" should have something a bit more definite in mind! She may depend on a ready-packaged pancake mix, frozen waffles, English muffins and coffee, or she may have a special dish at which she excels. If she can turn out appetizing French toast or a perfect omelet, if guests flocking into the kitchen won't upset her, she can be sure that friends will be glad to accept her spur-of-the-moment invitations.

I've never liked the word "brunch," but I must admit that many hostesses feel that it describes a "festive" breakfast. This is because in our modern days of constant rushing the average American thinks of juice, coffee and toast as a standard breakfast. The addition of cereal or eggs in any form is considered a very big breakfast indeed. As a child I always liked English stories because of the intriguing breakfasts so often described. There is something to be said in favor of rising a half hour earlier in order to eat a better breakfast, to relax over that piece of toast. But there is little point in giving etiquette rules for the average home at breakfast time, and the home in which there are servants is usually devoid of a breakfast rush.

Whether you are a career girl or a suburban matron, it is worthwhile to set the table for breakfast—even if you set it the night before. If, as is so often the case, different members of the family are ready for breakfast and must leave the house at various times, the buffet-type breakfast is your answer. This means a pitcher of juice, or possibly several glasses of juice ready on the serving counter or in the refrigerator (depending on the time span between first and last breakfast) and either a variety of cold packaged cereals or a double boiler of hot cereal, hot coffee, hot water, a pitcher of milk, toast or breakfast rolls or buns. If all can breakfast together, it is worth the extra effort to have eggs, French toast, waffles or pancakes occasionally. And whether you must have a serve-yourself meal or a more relaxed seated one, crisp grilled bacon, possibly sausages can do wonders to perk up a young appetite.

Although a damask or linen cloth may be used on the breakfast table, the place mat is far more popular. The table is laid for the number expected for breakfast with a service plate in the center of each place mat, and to the right, in the order in which used, a tea or orange spoon (for melon and such), cereal spoon, lunch-size knife. On the left of the service plate is a lunch-size fork. A bread-and-butter plate, with butter knife, should be above the fork, folded lunch-size napkin to the left of the fork. The water glass should be above the silver at the right of the plate. Naturally, if only cereal is served, the knife and fork are not at the place setting; if a juice is served, the orange spoon is not put down, nor is the cereal spoon on the table unless it will be needed. The coffee cup and saucer, with spoon on saucer, is brought in and placed at the right. If the coffee is poured at the table, the cups and saucers should be near the one who will pour and then pass it.

In homes of great wealth, it is not customary for ladies to eat breakfast in the dining room. In fact, in some such homes all breakfasts are served in the bedrooms. The guest in such a household may be asked when she wants her tray or requested to ring for it when ready. In the average home, however, guests should ascertain the breakfast hour and appear (fully dressed) to have breakfast with the family. Only very elderly ladies are allowed the luxury of coming to the dining room in negligee. Young women should *not* appear with hair in rollers, even if covered by a kerchief. "Dressed" means completely dressed.

The late Saturday or Sunday breakfast is an ideal way for the career man or woman to repay social obligations. This festive meal combines the good points of both breakfast and lunch—hence the coined word, "brunch." Although some hardy souls start such a meal with a round of drinks, I don't think too highly of the practice. It is not incorrect but certainly not very bright, since many of the guests will arrive sans even a cup of coffee! In addition, the food served is "light," usually a happy combination of breakfast and lunch menus. I suggest a juice or melon or grapefruit, followed by baked eggs, scrambled eggs, chipped beef, kippers, broiled or creamed chicken, possibly a souffle. This type of breakfast party may be a seated meal for four or it may be a buffet. If the former, the invitation should be for a specified hour. If the latter, the same rule may apply or the time allotted be told, as "Noon until two" or "Come between eleven and one."

10

*Dinners:
Formal and Informal*

TODAY MANY WELL-PLANNED, attractive dinner parties are possibly semi-formal but certainly not strictly formal. The hostess who can give a *really* formal seated dinner for ten or twelve can paraphrase the comment of the little girl who told her teacher that she didn't need to know anything about Europe because she could not afford to go there. Told that she might marry a wealthy man and travel through Europe, the youngster quickly replied that in that case she would not *need* to know the distance from Paris to London or how to get to Dublin, for she would hire somebody to take care of such details. So the hostess who can give such a lavish party either knows all the rules or has a butler, social secretary and competent domestic help, all of whom will know just what to do.

This chapter, therefore, is written mainly for the guest. The formal dinner is, above all, the place where the guest must show that he or she knows the correct thing to do.

Doubly so, for, the economics of formal entertaining being what they are, your host and hostess are more likely than not to be people of consequence—the Chairman of your Board, the President of your University, the Ambassador, the Admiral or the Senator. It may be an honor to attend, but it can be a disaster to offend.

Three forms of invitation are considered acceptable. The first is the traditional third-person invitation, which requires a formal third-person reply. The second is the short personal note, which may be answered in like manner or by telephone. Last, but by no means least, is the telephoned invitation, which is now entirely acceptable and which many modern hostesses find very satisfactory.

The prospective guest should remember these two points of etiquette: don't accept an invitation, then phone an excuse and decline because something more interesting has turned up. Be on time! Although some hostesses wait ten minutes, others go right ahead with dinner regardless of latecomers. When you consider that dinner invitations today always allow for at least a half hour of cocktails or aperitifs of some kind before dinner is announced, it seems very unlikely that anyone could be so tardy as to arrive after the other guests were seated. In this event, however, the latecomer goes directly to his hostess, murmurs a quick apology and takes his place at the table. Although some hostesses feel that he should start his meal from the first course, the more usual practice is for him to start with the course then on the table.

Meanwhile, back to the usual procedure at a formal dinner. A gentleman allows his wife to precede him into the drawing room. He gives their names to the footman on duty at the drawing room door. The servant may repeat them as "Mr. and Mrs. John Jones," but more often he announces "Mrs.

Jones, Mr. Jones." The hostess greets and shakes hands with each guest, then the host greets them and introduces them to other guests who are near. If the dinner is in honor of someone, the guest of honor stands with the host and hostess and each guest is presented by the hostess. From then until dinner is announced the guests mingle, chatting politely. It is not necessary for the hostess to make introductions at a formal dinner. Guests who are not acquainted introduce themselves. Although it is true that at a very large dinner the butler may stand at the opened door to the dining room or enter the drawing or living room and announce to the hostess "Dinner is served," it is far more usual for him to "catch the hostess' eye"; this signals that she should marshal her guests toward the dining room. At a very large dinner party there is a printed list for gentlemen to check and see whom they are to escort into dinner. However, many hostesses prefer the old-fashioned custom of presenting to a gentleman on arrival a silver tray of envelopes addressed to gentlemen guests. He selects his and on a small card within finds the name of the lady whom he is to take in to dinner. At a smaller party, the hostess may say "Dr. Jones, will you take Mrs. Brown," "I've put you next to Miss Dee, Mr. Black." The host then offers his right arm to the lady guest of honor and they lead the procession to the table, the others following, each lady on the right arm of her dinner companion. In smart social circles a man and wife are never seated together at dinner. However, at large professional or business dinners, especially if the guests have purchased tickets, the seating is decided by those at the table. Usually if a group takes a table, there is an order to their seating. If couples are seated at tables, sometimes with others whom they don't know, it is customary for each lady to sit with her escort. Such dinners, however, are really not "formal dinners," and there is no actual hostess.

In the dining room, the butler stands behind the hostess' chair, draws it out and helps her to be seated. At truly elaborate formal dinners, footmen do this for the lady guests. The usual procedure, however, is for each gentleman to draw out the chair and seat the lady whom he has escorted in to dinner. The lady guest of honor (or highest ranking lady) is on the host's right, with the next favored placed at the host's left. The gentleman guest of honor is on the hostess' right, the gentleman next in importance is placed on her left. Thus the less distinguished guests, family members or friends whom the hostess frequently sees are toward the middle of the table. (Since salt and pepper servers were placed at each end of the table, well in from the edge, the old expression "below the salt" implied one who was not of sufficient importance to be seated near the host or hostess.)

Let's face it, the logical reason for the hostess being the first served has, we trust, passed. (In the time of the Borgias the host tasted the food first to prove to his guests that there was no poison in it. This was later carried on to permit the hostess to "sample" the food to see that it was cooked to her satisfaction. Nowadays it is assumed that the cook or houseworker knows the food is properly cooked when it is sent to the table. And when did you ever see a hostess rise up in wrath, leave the table and go to the kitchen to reprimand the cook!) The usual custom is for service to start with the lady guest of honor, and the hostess is served in her turn. At small dinners it is usual to refrain from eating until all have been served. At a strictly formal dinner for more than six there is always a footman or waitress to serve four people. In this case, guests wait until those right around them have been served. Since in a well-run household the butler has the service thoroughly synchronized, this really amounts to all starting to eat at the same time.

After dessert, the hostess rises and precedes her guests to the drawing room. Demitasse and various liqueurs are there available. If there is no planned entertainment, such as cards or music, the guests remain only about a half hour after they have finished the coffee or liqueurs. It is no longer obligatory that guests wait until the guest of honor leaves. In saying good night guests usually say they enjoyed the evening, but it is not good form to extend an invitation to the hostess at that time.

In a club or hotel dining room one may decline a food, but this is never permissible in the hostess' own home. One on a diet or one who does not like a certain dish takes only a little on his plate and this may be left uneaten.

At a large party the "turning of the table" is still the sensible way to keep conversations alive. This means that the hostess talks a few minutes to the gentleman on her right, then turns and speaks with the gentleman on her left. Thus she "turns the flow of talk" and ladies alternate the conversation between the gentleman on either side. At a small dinner party conversation will be general at each end of the table, and there is no formal "turning" from right to left.

Although flowers are the standard center decorations, a rare piece of silver, fine porcelain figurines, pottery or pewter may also be used.

A white damask or fine lace cloth is still the favored choice for a formal dinner. However, embroidered or fine drawn-work place mats in white or pastel or pastel damask cloth and napkins are also acceptable for formal dining.

Formal dinners demand candles, which may be white or

in color to match the cloth but are always unshaded. Silver or crystal candlesticks or silver candelabra are the usual candle holders.

Most place cards are plain white or ivory cardboard. Sometimes a card is in a silver holder at each cover. More often it is folded (tent fashion) to stand up. It is permissible to use decorated cards (usually with hand-painted floral motifs), but they are not considered "smart." So, too, the hostess who has a family crest or a monogram stationery die may have her place cards engraved. Nowadays, however, this is considered a bit ostentatious. At a home dinner the names are handwritten, "Miss Smith" and "Mr. Jones." At a large business dinner they are sometimes typed and, if there are two or three with the same last name, the names appear as "Mr. John Jones," "Dr. Henry Brown."

At a large table, individual pepper and salt shakers are put at each place, centered above the place plate, or slightly larger shakers may be put down for every two places. At a table for no more than six or eight a larger set should be placed at each end of the table.

Whether the dinner is a very formal one or a quickly planned informal one, all spoons and knives are on the right of the place plate; all forks with the exception of the oyster fork are on the left. All silver is put down in the order in which it will be used, working in toward the plate. Dessert silver is always brought in with the dessert at a formal dinner; less formally, the dessert spoon and fork are put horizontally above the place plate. At a strictly formal dinner bread-and-butter plates are not used, nor is butter served. Today, however, many hostesses tend to break from this rule, and it is not surprising to find a dinner formally served in every way but with a bread-and-butter plate at each cover. (Each place at the table is referred to as a cover.)

Traditionally, all courses but the salad and dessert are served on matching china. The latter is often served on glass plates, or a special dessert plate in a different china pattern may be used. The hostess who has inherited beautiful china sometimes serves each course on a different pattern. This is now considered correct but, in my opinion, is only appropriate if the china is really beautiful and each pattern sufficiently different.

Obviously the hostess who has no maid or who must entertain with only the sporadic help of a day houseworker has a real challenge if she attempts a seated dinner. I have already pointed out that it is seldom feasible to have a seated dinner for more than six if you have only one maid. Actually, it is difficult for the average worker to cook the food, serve and clear the table, and be sure that all foods are served hot if she has more than four to wait on.

One important point to bear in mind is that in a maidless or one-maid household it is just not smart to serve more than five courses. The typical menu consists of fruit or shrimp cocktail, soup, a roast or roast poultry, salad, dessert. Although it is permissible to serve the salad with the main course (usually above and slightly to the left of the dinner plate), most hostesses prefer to keep it as a separate course. The advantage to a cold first course is that it can be on the table when dinner is announced. (It is never permissible to do this if hot soup is the first course.)

For this typical five-course dinner put a plate or service plate at each cover. The silver for the meal would be: on the right, a teaspoon or oyster fork, soup spoon, dinner knife. The knife, sharp edge turned in (toward the plate), should be about an inch from the plate. (All silver should be about that distance from the edge of the table.) To the left and farthest from the plate put the dinner fork, since it is used first, then the salad fork—next to the plate. A water goblet is above the knife, and when used, the bread-and-butter plate is above the fork. The butter knife, with handle toward the right, is across the bread-and-butter plate.

If the first course is on the table when guests sit down, the napkins should be next to the forks to the left of each service plate. Otherwise the napkins may be on the service plates. (The hostess who feels that her service plate center is too beautiful to hide may still put the napkin to the left, but it is considered "smarter" to put it on the plate.) Just before dinner is announced, the water glasses are filled—about three-quarters full, of course, not *brimming*.

The service rule is: Serve and remove everything from the left, except beverages, refilling of water glasses, and the addition of extra silver. These are all managed from the right. When there is only one maid, two soup plates may be brought in at once. She leaves one on the serving table until she has served the other. At the proper time (she either gauges or guesses it or the hostess discreetly rings for her) she re-enters the dining room and, going to the left of each place, picks up the soup plate and plate beneath and with her other hand puts down a warm plate for the main course. She repeats this at each cover until all hot main course plates are down. The meat is cut in the kitchen and the maid serves it on a platter held on her open hand. (It is usually necessary for her to have a small service napkin on the hand as a protection against heat.) After all have been served meat, she leaves the platter on the serving table and brings in two vegetable dishes or a two-compartment dish (for a small group). The vegetables are passed in the same way as the meat. After the meat course plates are removed, the individual salad plates are put down. (Each cover is serviced at one time—the plate picked up, salad plate put down.)

As the salad plates are removed with the right hand, the bread-and-butter plates are picked up with the left hand, thus clearing the cover. Then all extra silver and the salt and pepper shakers are removed. If necessary the table is very unobtrusively crumbed, water glasses are refilled—and all is in readiness for dessert.

At a strictly formal dinner, desserts are usually served on glass dessert plates. Occasionally, however, individual desserts are brought in either in sherbet glasses or cups. In either case there is a glass plate beneath. In hotels and sometimes at very large home dinners, the finger bowls are brought in when the dessert is finished. In this case the dessert is removed with the left hand and, with the right hand, the finger bowl (on a plate and correctly with a doily beneath) is put down. At smaller dinners, the finger bowl, doily and small plate are sometimes brought in on the dessert plate. Each guest picks up the small plate containing doily and finger bowl and puts it on his left. This leaves the dessert plate ready for use. In a home service, when individual desserts are served, it is customary to bring in the finger bowls before the dessert, but the hostess who prefers may follow the hotel method.

At a professional, business or other large organization dinner service is just the same as at any formal dinner. The only difference is that there usually are speakers; frequently there is a special dais where the speakers, honored guests and officers are seated. The chairman sits in the center of the dais with the most important speaker on his right, next one in importance on his left, and so on. At the end of the dinner, frequently after the dessert and coffee are at each place, the chairman (or toastmaster) rises and makes a few opening remarks. He then introduces the first speaker of the evening. After the first speaker sits down, the chairman rises again, thanks him and introduces the second speaker; and so on. The guest of honor or most important speaker is always the last to speak. Usually the chairman says a few brief words of appreciation and the dinner is officially over.

11

Lunches:
Formal and Informal

WEBSTER'S DICTIONARY LISTS both "lunch" and "luncheon," but the former is the choice of those who are well bred. Social climbers extend invitations to luncheon but the word seems ostentatious to most of us, so whether it is to be a simple meal cooked and served by the hostess or an exotic but light repast prepared by a French chef and served by a butler, in conservative society it is "lunch."

In England and on the Continent it is not unusual for men to go home to lunch or to take time for a lunch party in home surroundings. In this country, however, most men have lunch in restaurants that cater to business and professional people or in private clubs. Hence when we think of the midday meal we think of a woman's gathering. This chapter, then, is not for the business or professional men or career women who eat with contemporaries and who need only be guided by the usual rules for good table manners and conduct in restaurants. It is intended for the woman who entertains at lunch at home, whether in town or country. One need hardly add, however, that business or professional careers *may* be very much at stake in such apparently innocent feminine gatherings.

For the average large party, the usual invitation is a large visiting card or "informal" on which is written "lunch" and the date, hour and place. If it is to be followed by cards or a fashion show of any kind, this should be indicated. Otherwise, some non-card-playing guests are bound to feel trapped. The telephoned invitation is the accepted one for small (often not so small) parties.

It should not be necessary to remind the reader that an invitation to a lunch, like any invitation, requires a reply.

One o'clock is the usual time, but if cocktails are to be served first the invitations should be for twelve-thirty. Allow a half hour for drinks, an hour for the meal. Unless cards or a show follow, the guests should all leave before three. Those who have appointments or are going to a matinee may leave as soon as lunch is over. At a large lunch guests who must leave early may go directly from the table—having first said good-by to and thanked the hostess. (Those who leave any party early should try to make their departure as inconspicuous as possible.)

In smart social groups a lunch guest does *not* take a gift to her hostess. In some communities, especially in rural and suburban settings, this is customary. The newcomer in a community should ascertain the local custom on this score.

At an informal lunch ladies wear simple afternoon dresses, suits or spectator-sport dresses. A formal lunch is really gala, and one's best bib-and-tucker are in order. It is well to remember that hats are always correct at lunch. Prior to the Second World War all ladies wore hats, and it was not unusual for a very dignified hostess to put on her own hat even though the lunch was in her home. Nowadays half the guests at an informal lunch may arrive hatless, but it is to be hoped that even those who don't like hats will don bandeaux, flat ribbon bows or some form of headgear for a really formal lunch. Needless to say, it is not necessary for the hostess or house guests to wear hats at a home lunch.

Whether the lunch is formal or informal, the hostess does not have to remain standing until all guests arrive. She rises when a lady enters, shakes hands and introduces her to guests near.

If men are present at a formal lunch they may wear either morning clothes, a stroller jacket and striped trousers, or a dark business suit. The latter is the usual choice in most sections of the country and in most social circles. For an informal lunch, men wear business suits, conservative sport clothes or, in summer, light slacks and blazers. Unless it is an out-and-out country or beach setting, they wear white shirts and appropriate ties.

Gentlemen who are present at lunch do not escort ladies to the table, nor is there any formal "going in to lunch" as there is to dinner. A man may walk in with whomever he is talking with when lunch is announced, or all men present may wait and follow the ladies in.

No matter how formal the lunch, it is never as stately as a dinner. Everything is light; the talk should be bright and gay. It is, in short, a "fun" time.

At a very big party it is necessary to have several tables. For a party for less than twenty, most hostesses prefer one big table since this lends itself to general conversation and seems more intimate and friendly.

Although a lace or fine embroidered sheer cloth may be used, the popular choice for lunch is the bare table with place mats. These may be lace, fine linen, one of the synthetics, or novelty cork, braid or plastic.

Candles are never used on the lunch table. Floral or other decorations are usually used as a centerpiece.

Unless it is a very big lunch, place cards are not used. When they are needed, plain white and ivory are preferred, although gaily decorated ones are sometimes used for special occasions. The place card may be centered directly above the place plate or, especially if the first course is on the table, they may be to the left of the plate—usually above the napkin.

The plates, napkins and silverware used at lunch are smaller than those at dinner and are commonly referred to as "lunch plates," "lunch knives and forks" and so on. The lunch napkin is always folded in a triangle, and when placed on the table the long side of the triangle is next and parallel to the forks.

Although the formal lunch may consist of five courses, four-course lunches are more popular, with the three-course lunch favored by the hostess who has no maid. The no-knife lunch, which had been very much in vogue several years ago, is now considered the ideal for a buffet lunch but is seldom encountered at a sit-down serviced meal.

For the standard lunch, the place plate is in the center of each cover, with the lunch knife and a spoon (for consomme or fruit cup) or small fork (for sea food cocktail) to the right. To the left of the plate are the forks, the salad one next the plate, lunch fork to the left of it.

It is usual to bring in dessert silver with the dessert but, if preferred, the continental service may be used—the dessert silver is then placed above the place plate, usually with the spoon handle on the right, fork handle on the left.

For a no-knife lunch—since there is no knife but the butter

one, which as at all meals is on the bread-and-butter plate to the left of the place plate—the lunch and salad forks are put down to the right of the plate—in the order in which they will be used.

Although it is naturally much simpler in every way, the service for lunch is the same as that for dinner (see Chapter 10).

Coffee is seldom served at the lunch table. The hostess usually has it (tea also, if possible) available in the living room. At a business or large, fairly impersonal lunch, if time must be considered, the coffee may be (*quietly*) served at the table while the business or club report is read or discussed.

Mr. and Mrs. John Henry Dee

Miss Jane Elizabeth Doe

Mrs. Henry David Jones

PLATE I A selection of the family's visiting cards shown in the actual sizes.

Mr. John Joseph Smith

Mr and Mrs John Avery Booth

request the honour of your presence

at the marriage of their daughter

Nancy Marie

to

Mr David Albert Charles Kelly

on Saturday, the second of March

at four o'clock

Saint Peter's Church

Essex Fells, New Jersey

The pleasure of your company

is requested at the reception

immediately following the ceremony

Montclair Golf Club

Montclair

R.s.v.p.
117 Forest Way
Essex Fells

Wedding Breakfast

immediately following the ceremony

The St. Regis Roof

R.s.v.p.
Four East Seventy-second Street

PLATE II The large card is a standard form of invitation to attend a church wedding ceremony. Accompanying it may be one of the smaller cards extending an invitation to attend the reception or, alternatively, a wedding breakfast.

Mr. and Mrs. Myron Arms Wick, Jr.

request the pleasure of your company

at the wedding reception of their daughter

Wendy

and

Mr. William Johnson Evans

on Saturday, the fourteenth of September

at half after five o'clock

Cherry Valley Road

Greenwich, Connecticut

R.s.v.p.

PLATE III   Equally correct is the form and engraving of this invitation to attend a church wedding. In this case the larger card is the invitation to the reception and the smaller the invitation to the ceremony.

The honour of your presence is requested

at the marriage ceremony

at five o'clock

Round Hill Community Church

Please present this card at

The Southport Congregational Church

on Saturday, the twenty-fourth of June

PLATE IV   The church seat card is seldom used save in the case of very large weddings involving prominent people.

Mrs. William Penn White

has the honour of announcing

the marriage of her daughter

Patricia White Van Wyck

to

Mr. Clayton Adelbert Farrar

on Saturday, the eleventh of January

Nineteen hundred and sixty-four

Montclair, New Jersey

PLATE V   The correct form
for an announcement of her
daughter's wedding sent by a
widow.

Doctor and Mrs. Frederick Thomas Edmunds

will be at home

after the tenth of November

1507 Virginia Street, East

Charleston, West Virginia

Mr. and Mrs. Thomas Brooke Price

have the honour of announcing

the marriage of their daughter

Caroline

to

Doctor Frederick Thomas Edmunds

on Saturday, the eighteenth of October

Nineteen hundred and fifty-eight

in the Chapel of

Saint Peter's Church

Morristown, New Jersey

PLATE VI An "At
Home" card and a stand-
ard announcement, both
showing the correct form
for professional titles.

PLATE VIII Illustrated here are a variety of table linens and basic service accessories that might be used for formal entertaining.

PLATE IX Basic equipment for a formal place setting includes (left to right) soup plate, claret glass, wine glass, goblet, soup bowl, butter plate, cup and saucer, dinner plate, spoon, soup spoon, butter knife, salad fork, fork and knife. To this could be added a place plate, special silver such as an oyster fork (which would be set on the extreme right) or a fish fork (set on the extreme left) and several special styles of wine glasses.

PLATE X   An informal table setting for
lunch.

PLATE XI   This table is set for a semi-
formal lunch. There will be a soup course
but no salad or wine.

PLATE XII   This setting for a formal lunch
at home or a professional lunch in the office
indicates three courses (soup, main, salad),
dessert and a single wine.

PLATE XIII A typical setting for informal late-afternoon tea. At the far end of the table are a sherry decanter and glasses.

PLATE XIV   A semi-formal setting for a
dinner: two courses, dessert and wine.

PLATE XV A setting for a formal dinner.
The order of silver indicates four courses
(appetizer, soup, main, salad). A single
wine is being served.

PLATE XVI   In the semi-buffet, the dinner table is set as for a regular dinner party
except that plates are stacked on the serving
table or sideboard.

PLATE XVII A typical arrangement for a buffet supper. On the serving table are all the necessary silver, china and linen for each guest. Crystal will be set forth on a separate table or will be brought to the guests later.

12

Teas, Receptions
and Card Parties

FORMAL AFTERNOON TEA parties are not as popular now as in former years. This is possibly due to the increased popularity of cocktail parties and the fact that it is far easier to persuade men to attend them or to "stop in for a drink about six" than to agree to attend a tea.

However, as a means of bringing together the members of a charitable committee, as a way to bring company wives together or a way to arouse interest in a community project, the formal tea is in many ways ideal.

It is considered an honor to be asked to "pour" at a formal tea. Unlike the informal tea, which is poured by the hostess in the living room, the dining room or a refectory table is the setting for the formal tea trays. A lady sits at each end of the oblong table. One has a complete tea service on a tray, the other presides over the coffee service, also on a tray. Silver services are traditional, but china pots, with a fancy metal kettle of hot water, sugar bowl, cream pitcher, plate of lemon slices, and a supply of small plates, cups and saucers, and tea or cocktail napkins, will suffice if necessary. In this case tole trays would have to substitute for the decorative and impressive silver ones. Since it is a formal party, ladies who "pour" wear hats or some form of headgear, be it ever so fragile or tiny. At this type of tea, especially if many of the guests will stand, only "dry" tea sandwiches and simple cookies or small pieces of pound or other not-too-crumbly cake should be served, since each guest will put her sandwich or cake on the saucer next to her cup.

With the exception of a centerpiece, usually of flowers, there is nothing on the table, but plates of sandwiches and cookies, near each tray. The table may be covered with a lace or sheer cloth or, more popular at present, may be uncovered.

Guests go to the table, ascertain which lady has tea or coffee, and take their cups either back to where they had been sitting or, if chairs are at a premium, walk a little away from the table to avoid blocking the refreshment area. Obviously a lady who can't find a chair does not complicate things for herself by taking a cake plate for her sandwich or cookie.

If the formal tea follows a meeting, guests leave any time after they have had refreshments. If it is intended as a way of bringing a group together, guests stay at the tea thirty to forty minutes.

If, as is usually the case, the tea lasts more than an hour, teams of ladies pour. Thus no lady is deprived of meeting with and talking to others, since her tea table duties last only about a half hour.

The more usual tea party—and it is regaining some of its former popularity—is the informal tea at which the hostess presides over the tea tray. This, as I have already mentioned, is served in the living room. No matter how wealthy the home, a servant is never present at an informal tea. If the hostess needs more hot water, cakes or a new supply of cups and saucers she rings and, when the maid enters, tells her what is needed.

The tea tray (heirloom silver, we hope, but a wicker tray with a good china pot will suffice) is placed on the tea table in front of the hostess. Guests seated near her accept their cups without rising; those a little distance away or across the room go to her for their tea. Each guest picks up a folded napkin and a plate and helps herself to sandwiches, toast, cake or cookies from the small table or muffin stand next to the tea table, then, with tea that the hostess pours and gives to her, returns to her place.

The tea tray always contains cream as well as lemon slices, and the guest who prefers cream should say so. Less often, in addition to cut sugar, a sugar substitute is available.

A fine white cloth is the usual choice for the tea table, but pastel-colored ones are equally correct. Dark tones or plaids are, of course, not used.

A very dignified hostess once remarked that the most important thing at a tea is plenty of hot water. To that I would add "a good supply of occasional tables." When we realize the wide variety of folding and collapsible tables now available, it seems ridiculous that any hostess should expect guests to manage cake plate, cup and saucer, napkin—possibly even a *fork*—without a table surface on which to put them. As I mentioned in reference to formal tea parties, lacking sufficient chairs and small tables, food should be limited to dry compact cakes and sandwiches.

The English "high tea" is seldom encountered in this country, but it does have its adherents. This differs from the standard informal tea only in variety and richness of foods. It is always a small party, and occasional tables are essential. Foods are such things as chicken patty shells, waffles, rolled thin pancakes with deviled ham, cottage cheese or sour cream filling and a gourmet pie or layer cake in addition to the usual tea party fare.

Men are seldom present at tea but when they are they first get tea and cakes for ladies in their group or near them and then take tea to ladies a distance from the tea table.

What to wear depends on one's social group and activities. A formal tea calls for an afternoon dress or dressmaker suit, hat, white gloves. For an informal tea, one would wear one's usual attire at that hour—a simple dress, tailored suit, a hat if one usually wears one. Obviously slacks and shorts should only be worn in the country and then at a very informal tea given by a close friend.

At a formal tea, gentlemen wear dark business suits unless they belong to a very social and old-fashioned group or on that day have reason to wear morning clothes or stroller jackets. Business suits or conservative slacks and jackets or blazers might be worn to an informal tea and, in the country, casual clothes usually worn in public at that time in the day would be permissible. Obviously, no matter how casual the attire, a gentleman would wear a jacket or blazer.

A reception is rather similar to a formal tea although there are some differences and variations. The most important difference is that there must be a *reason* for a reception, whereas a hostess can give a tea, formal or informal, any time she so desires. A reception is given in honor of a new minister, a distinguished citizen, a newcomer in the community, or one who has received an honor or prize of some kind. A reception is often given for a new bride or a bride and bridegroom who, married elsewhere, have returned to a home town. It is not unusual to have a reception in honor of a recently engaged girl, but if the engagement is to be *announced* at an afternoon party it is more usual to invite guests to a formal tea and, at it, make the announcement.

Another way in which the reception differs is that maids or caterer's men are always present during a reception. They serve the guests, pass around the room with refreshments. At a very large and formal reception the servants handle the buffet or a service bar, and champagne—sometimes liquors —are available in addition to the tea and coffee. In addition, there is a greater variety of light foods available, often bouillon, individual salads, tea sandwiches or patties, ice cream, champagne wafers or macaroons, and tea and coffee.

The hostess stands with the guest of honor; those who don't know her are presented to her by the hostess. Her acquaintances greet her and offer congratulations if they are in order. Having "paid their respects" to hostess and honored guest, they mingle with others present, partake of refreshments, and so on. As in the case of a formal dinner, it is no longer necessary for all other guests to remain until the guest of honor leaves.

For both men and women, attire is the same as for a formal tea.

Card parties, although predominantly afternoon gatherings, are not quite the same as receptions and teas. Yet in recent years more and more women have turned to afternoon card parties as a way of entertaining. However, we must bear in mind that the card party places a special obligation on the guests—they must be able to play bridge or canasta or the favored game of their community.

One who can't play cards should not accept an invitation to a "lunch bridge" or "dessert bridge" because the main reason for the gathering is card playing. However, many charitable groups plan an all-embracing party for their cause and the ticket includes lunch, cards and a fashion show or bazaar. With this as an inducement, the non-card playing lady who "takes a table" or merely buys a ticket need only plan to "skip" the card session or use the time for playing some form of table games or just "chatting" with other non-players, but in tones too low to disturb serious card players.

Whether it is a private party or a large benefit, a well-bred guest neither boasts about *nor* belittles her playing before the game. When playing starts, she doesn't depreciate her hand nor gloat over it. One should resist the temptation to hold a postmortem after the game and remember—a graceful winner is as important as a graceful loser.

Don't talk too much! One who takes the game seriously will be irritated by a gay, chattering tablemate. Don't put purse, gloves and so on on the corner of the table. This kind of clutter can be distracting.

The hostess' obligations consist in inviting players of about equal skill, or at least making up her tables with the guests' playing ability in mind. She should see that there are two packs of fresh cards and a score pad and two pencils on each table. If—as one would presume, since it is a "party"—there are several tables, there should be a card on each table, listing the players assigned there.

This, of course, is optional, but most hostesses put cigarets, matches, an ash tray and a small dish of candy on each table. If these seem to crowd the table, eliminate part or all of the "luxury" touch.

The hostess should never suggest playing for stakes unless she knows that this is at least agreeable to her guests. Obviously she should not invite anyone to this kind of game if she has any doubt about the prospective guest's views on the subject or financial position. One who inadvertently finds herself faced with a game she feels she can't or does not want to afford should say so at once.

If a club or group makes a practice of giving high score prize and it is won by a "guest" or "substitute" player, it is usually given (even if "reluctantly") to the guest. Those who want to avoid such a situation should have a lesser "guest" prize. It is unthinkable that a guest who wins should go home with no form of prize.

As I have previously mentioned, there is no rule against men attending afternoon parties, but they themselves prefer to be conspicuous by their absence. Also, although men like to play cards, they prefer just one table if it is a mixed group and, even when only men play in a smoke-filled room, they avoid a "card session" as big as the average "charity" card gatherings. Thus the Monday-to-Friday afternoon social activities of this kind are confined to the ladies. Whether the game is in her own home or a club, the hostess should terminate it well before six o'clock. The average man does not like to come home to find the place filled with afternoon guests. He *does* like to find his wife there when he arrives, however. The interval between Dad's arrival home and dinner is usually considered "family time." In the suburbs especially this is often the only time when the family can be together. Thus guests who enjoyed a pleasant afternoon should take their departure before six and not let the afternoon run over into the evening.

13

Informal Parties

BECAUSE MANY OF us are inclined to think that, with enough money, anyone can give a successful party, I want to stress here that the best hostess is not necessarily the one who spends the most. True and real hospitality is not just elaborate entertaining. To be a good hostess you must want to entertain your friends, must take an interest in all the details that make your particular party a success.

You may not be able to give a seated dinner for eight, but you may be able to give a very informal Sunday breakfast party. One of the main things to remember is that everyone should enjoy a party—this means the hostess, too. You don't want to look worried and tense, so don't attempt a party that is too big or too elaborate for you. The first thing to decide is the kind of party you can give. This means you must consider the space available, the silver, china and glassware that you have, can borrow or rent. (Rented equipment is no longer frowned upon. In this day of small storage space and streamlined living it is a boon to the hostess. Look into the possibility of renting such things as tables, chairs, silver, linens and so on before you make your final party plans.)

In planning parties for children or young adults, it is advisable to limit the guest list to a given age group. It just is not possible to have five-year-old youngsters at the party for a thirteen-year-old boy. Their interests aren't the same. On the other hand, I find that in planning a party for adults one should really "mix" the guests. A twenty-year-old who likes serious music can be happy discussing opera with those three times her age. The thirty-year-old lawyer can find a fifty-year-old newspaperman a good conversationalist.

A party for small children should be small in number of guests, too. The guests should be the child's closest friends, the tots she plays with in playground or park. Although some mothers give afternoon birthday parties for pre-school and first-grade children, I really think a few children invited to lunch or supper at which the birthday cake is served is a more sensible arrangement. Many mothers frown on between-meal eating and feel that ice cream and cake in late afternoon spoil the child's appetite for supper. The children should play games they know, and each little guest should receive a souvenir or tiny gift to take home, since youngsters in this age group are too young to enjoy contests or vie for prizes.

The ten-year-old is entitled to a birthday or holiday party for his friends. At this age he should decide whom he wants to invite, and it is not necessary for Mother to know the guests. In addition, he should *not* be told it is his party, then find that he is expected to invite the children of his parents' friends whom he does not know.

Mid-afternoon is the popular party time for the grade school group. At this age they usually enjoy games, contests and prizes. They seldom, however, enjoy mixed groups, so don't insist that the ten- or eleven-year-old boy invite little girls to his party. Girls, too, are happiest to have their girl classmates and other friends but are ill at ease with boys.

The children in the grade school group (from about seven or eight to eleven or twelve) may have a lunch or supper party, but, as I mentioned, they themselves prefer afternoon ones. This simplifies matters for the hostess. A typical snack menu for such a party could be small sandwiches, potato chips, pretzels, ice cream, birthday or special holiday cake, or assorted cookies and soft drinks. Unless the party is given outdoors, please don't assume that the children will drink directly from the bottles! A party is a party—even for a tousled-haired small boy.

The most important thing to remember in planning a party for high school girls and boys is that there must be adults present (not actually "in the room" but definitely in adjoining rooms). Apart from sensible supervision and a co-operative attitude on the part of the youngster who gives the party, there is not too much work for parents in a teenage gathering. At this age they have definite and very set notions about what to serve, what music to play, and the other points that to normal well-trained youngsters will seem important. Few young people in this group like "surprise" entertainment. Since they know what they like and whom they want to invite, the party requires less adult planning. There should, however, be some form of music and some space for dancing. Cards or some kind of games should also be available if wanted. What games to offer will depend on where you live. Few apartment dwellers can have darts, ping pong or parlor golf, yet these are fine for a suburban home.

Most of these "mixed" high school parties are held at night, but they should, of course, end far earlier than the party for adults. In most respects, however, the teenage party is the same as the average party for older people. One word of caution: it is not enough to serve only soft drinks, the alert hostess must see to it that no young guest brings in liquor. By watching in this regard and a firm rule against "crashers," the parents of a teenager can be good hosts and also see that the party never gets out of hand.

We all have birthdays, but not all of us like to have them celebrated. However, the all-over most popular form of party is still the birthday celebration. There are two kinds, the "known" and the "surprise" party. The former is often given by, as many Europeans say, "the birthday child" (this, regardless of the age of the "child"). Obviously a party in honor of a birthday should be planned on what the guest of honor likes in the way of entertainment. Such a party may be big or small, may be given at home or may be in the form of dinner in a restaurant, attendance at a theater or sport event, or a combination of dinner-and-a-theater or lunch followed by the ball game or popular tennis matches.

No matter what the age, gifts are in order. For this reason, in planning a surprise party, tell the guests so that they won't feel embarrassed to arrive without gifts and find it is a birthday party.

Whether the birthday is for a school child or an adult, gifts should be opened during the party and givers thanked. If possible, a thank-you note should be sent later. Such a note must be sent if one receives a gift from someone who does not attend the party and therefore can't be thanked in person.

It is impossible to list appropriate gifts, since there are so many that such a list would be almost endless. Suffice to point out that men don't give wearing apparel to women unless close relatives. Nor may a woman give wearing apparel to a non-related man.

Regardless of the age and also even if the one who is being honored seems to scoff at birthday cakes, a cake of some sort is in order. In the case of those under twenty-one, if the cake is big enough there may be a candle for each year plus one "to grow on." If the cake is small, and *always* for those over twenty-one, there are three candles—for health, wealth and happiness.

Although in some communities special attention is paid and an elaborate party given for a girl's sixteenth birthday, a "sweet sixteen" party is not considered in best taste. In conservative circles it does not differ from any other birthday party. Certainly such a party should end at a reasonable hour, no liquor should be served and a girl of that age should not then be treated as a grownup.

Whether the couple "celebrates" their wedding anniversary by going out to dinner and a theater, whether they plan a reunion with their honor attendant and best man, or have a real party with as many of the original wedding guests as they can muster and their relatives and present friends, a wedding anniversary is usually celebrated. Certainly a yearly anniversary celebration is a good habit, draws the couple and their family closer together.

Having settled on having a party, the next point to consider is, should it be an informal gathering at home—strictly a "fun" evening—or should it be a formal renewal of vows, possibly before a clergyman and in church? Should this serious remembrance of the wedding be followed by an informal party or a formal one, possibly in hotel or restaurant?

If you decide on the latter, the first thing to do is to make the proper arrangements with the clergyman. Roman Catholics frequently consider the fitting celebration is the mass, followed by reception of communion and renewal of the wedding vows, and this religious ceremony is followed by a typical "wedding breakfast" complete with bride's cake.

With the exception of the informal home party, which is usually an evening gathering, the anniversary party, like a wedding reception, may be in the form of a luncheon, tea (actually a cocktail party), dinner or an evening party with dancing. A buffet supper is usually served at the latter. In each case the only unusual feature of the menu is the bride's cake, which often has the wedding date and names on the icing.

Some couples hold a "mock wedding," with the original bridal party if possible. Some women like to don their bridal dresses for anniversary parties. Although both of these are permissible, I personally feel that if one doesn't have a religious ceremony of some kind, a dignified celebration party, without "gimmicks," is the better choice.

As in the case of a birthday party, guests who realize the reason for the gathering always bring or send gifts. Although the first anniversary is considered the paper or plastic one, the second, cotton and so on, it is not mandatory that the gift be of the "appropriate" material or composition for the specific year. The exception is in the case of the tenth (tin or aluminum) and twenty-fifth, which is known as the "silver anniversary." In these cases, the gift usually "goes" with the anniversary. For other years it is equally correct, and often more interesting, to buy what seems appropriate for the particular couple and carry out the theme in the wrapping or decorating of the package. Thus a gift for the seventh anniversary could be wrapped in copper-colored paper, a lace handkerchief might decorate the package for the thirteenth, and so on.

The first five anniversaries are usually treated comically.

After the fifteenth there is only a special meaning for every fifth year.

Wedding Anniversaries

1st	Paper-Plastic	13th	Lace
2nd	Cotton	14th	Ivory
3rd	Linen	15th	Crystal
4th	Silk	20th	China
5th	Wood	25th	Silver
6th	Iron	30th	Pearl
7th	Copper	35th	Coral
8th	Bronze	40th	Ruby
9th	Pottery	45th	Sapphire
10th	Tin-Aluminum	50th	Gold
11th	Steel	55th	Emerald
12th	Silk-Nylon	75th	Diamond

It is not necessary to decorate the party rooms, but it lends a touch of gaiety. For those who want to do so white satin ribbons or paper streamers, white crepe paper, tinsel, paper wedding bells, cupids, heart cutouts may be used. Personally, I prefer a vase or two of fresh flowers.

If you want to hold your party—whether to celebrate a birthday, an anniversary or for some other special reason—in a hotel or restaurant, make your reservations and arrangements well in advance. Select the room, location of table, and menu. (If possible, arrange to have a choice of main course.) Most hotels, restaurants and "halls" require a down payment at least; some want the major part of the bill paid in advance. In either case, if the tips are not included in the bill, it is well to give the headwaiter the gratuities for your waiters at that time. This eliminates the waiters' worry that they won't be tipped and usually insures good service.

Short personal notes, telephone calls or gaily printed "fun" invitations may be issued for informal parties. Whether it is a birthday party for a school child or an anniversary party for your parents, be sure that each prospective guest is *really* invited. You can't depend on your child to deliver verbal invitations in school—and some mothers won't permit their youngsters to accept invitations extended in this fashion. You can't tell Aunt Jane to tell Aunt Alice that she is invited, unless they live in the same house and are invited as a unit. In this case the telephoned invitation is given to the one who answered the phone.

Wedding anniversary celebrations that have a religious or dignified aspect require formal invitations. These may be printed for the occasion, or engraved invitation cards with blank spaces to be filled in may be used.

It goes without saying that all who receive a party invitation of any kind have an obligation to acknowledge it as promptly as possible.

A party may be in a smart restaurant, in the hostess' small living room, or in a gaily decorated cellar rumpus room. No matter where it is held, or what is served, a gracious hostess is the most important ingredient for a successful party.

14

Dances and Balls

FEW OF US go through life without attending at least one
dance. Naturally not all are good dancers, but we should all
be able to dance well enough to avoid stepping on a partner's
feet. It is not necessary to be able to do all the latest and
novelty dances, but one who can't dance well enough to get
by should take a few lessons or ask a patient relative or
friend for help in practicing basic steps.

When we think of dancing, we think first of young people.
Dancing and dances can give happiness to young men and
women and can also be the cause of much unhappiness. This
is especially true of those who lack poise, who have no self-
confidence. So the reader who feels inadequate in a ballroom
needs to brush up on his dancing *and* his social poise. As a
psychologist said recently, "It is healthy fun for the young.
Keeps the middle aged feeling young and the old feeling
middle aged." In addition, the ability to dance, like other
social assets, is a help in making new friends, in widening
one's social circle.

The ballroom dancing classes of our childhood may not have been "fun sessions," but the girl who went to dancing school learned to walk across a dance floor with grace, the boy there learned the fundamentals of social courtesy and chivalry. There are still some middle-aged men who know how to "offer the right arm" to a lady as they walk into a ballroom, still some young women who know how to promenade across the dance floor. The vast majority of us, however, have forgotten or never knew how to enter a ballroom. Thus we see the girl stride well ahead of her escort, possibly clutch him as the signal that she's ready to dance. We see a prospective dance partner with his hand in his pocket as he slouches after her. (Too many young men nowadays seem to think that one hand in a dinner jacket or trousers pocket signifies great sophistication and self-assurance!)

What is the difference between a dance and a ball? The former is for a special group and all guests have common interests or are in the same age bracket. The latter is for everybody—young and old. Although a few hostesses of great wealth can afford to give a private ball, most balls nowadays are galas for charitable causes, often yearly events at which some debutantes are introduced or there is some special yearly motif. The ball that is noted for its debutantes is public but only on a subscription basis. The spectacular charity ball is open to the general public—usually at a substantial fee, which is donated to charity.

There's another difference between a dance and a ball: at the former ladies may wear simple, even short—when they are fashionable—dance dresses and gentlemen may wear dinner jackets. A ball, on the other hand, calls for formal attire; the ladies wear elaborate ball gowns and gentlemen wear evening clothes (white tie and tails).

At present corsages are not very fashionable, but let us

hope this is temporary, for the custom of sending a corsage to one's "dance date" is a gracious one.

A dance that is planned for young people should have chaperons. These may be listed as "Members of the Dance Committee," "Sponsors" or "Patrons." The title is not important, but the ladies should be briefed on what is expected of them. A "Floor Committee," made up of older boys or men, is a good addition to the chaperons' ranks.

If the dance or ball is sponsored by a girl's club or school, the girl asks a man to escort her and she supplies the tickets or invitations. He pays the other expenses of the evening. The tactful course is for the girl to give her escort the tickets or "bids" before they start out. This avoids her fumbling for them at the entrance. (This sort of thing always makes a man feel either ill at ease or furious!)

The private dance, whether in a home, club or hotel, is always by invitation only. The hostess who plans such a party must be careful to see that all who should be invited receive invitations. In a big city an omission may not be overly serious, but in the suburbs it can be disastrous to overlook an eligible. (You just don't snub "those in your group" in the suburbs, for it can start a social feud.) It is always permissible to borrow a friend's guest list if you don't personally know enough people to invite. Frankly, if I didn't know them, I would not want to invite them. The only time when this would be understandable to me is when planning a dance for young people. It would be fine to invite the friends of the sons of one's contemporaries. The only disadvantage to this is that when you have too many guests whom you don't personally know things may get a bit out of hand.

It is always permissible (and usually appreciated) if you telephone a hostess and ask permission to bring an extra man or suggest that he be invited. Extra men are always welcome at dances. An extra girl, however, can create a problem, and unless you can be sure she knows enough young men who will attend or can bring her own escort, don't embarrass a hostess by suggesting the addition of another girl. It is also not tactful to ask the hostess to invite someone she herself knows. She may have a reason for not sending an invitation.

One who receives an invitation through the suggestion of a friend should, if possible, arrive at the dance with the one who "sponsored" him. If he must arrive alone he should say to his hostess "So and So asked if I might come" or "John Doe asked you to invite me." The hostess extends her hand and says, "I'm so glad you could come."

The time a dance starts varies. In most big cities ten o'clock is the usual hour. In smaller communities or when the dance is for a younger group nine o'clock is preferred. Most of us hate to be the first to arrive, but it is silly to wait until eleven when the invitation states "Ten o'clock." When you consider that the hostess must pay for the orchestra from the time specified it is unrealistic for her guests to purposely delay, then often try to cajole the orchestra leader to play "one more number" at the end of the evening.

In planning a dance the hostess or committee must bear in mind that the music plays a very important part in the success of the evening. For this reason great care should be taken in engaging an orchestra. It is well to remember, also, that an orchestra that usually plays for older or more conservative groups will not be appreciated by a very young crowd unless the orchestra can adapt the rhythm or beat to suit the youngsters.

It is no longer considered obligatory for a man to ask a girl to dance when he is introduced to her. However, if a member of the Floor Committee or a hostess asks him to "Come meet Jane Smith. Her partner is rather neglectful" he has no choice but to accept the introduction and ask the girl to dance. However, if he is escorting another girl he may, after once or twice around the floor, say he has to return to his date and ask if he can take his current partner to her friends. If she is smart, she won't let him stay with her that long. Once away from the hostess, she'll tactfully ask him to excuse her or say she wants to make a phone call.

Dance etiquette has passed through several phases in the twentieth century. Prior to the First World War each girl cherished her "dance program." The young man who, early in the evening, asked to see her program and wrote his name in for several dances was thereupon considered a real beau. At college dances it was chivalrous for a girl's escort to "fill" her program by asking his friends to write in their names. In those days a gentleman checked his program, went to the lady, and said "I believe this dance is mine?" She acquiesced and preceded him to the dance floor.

This era was followed by the period of "open choice," when at the start of a dance the gentleman asked a lady "May I have this dance?" She answered "Yes, of course" or "Thank you" or merely smiled and accompanied him out on the floor. At the end of the dance, he returned her to her group, thanked her and, unless his leaving would mean she was then alone, looked for another partner.

During this period the "cut-in" system started. In this it is permissible for a man to tap the shoulder of another who is dancing as a sign that he wants to "cut in" or take the dancer's partner. A man may not refuse to be cut in on, but his partner may smilingly decline. However, this is only customary if she is dancing with her fiance, husband or father. It is hardly smart for a girl to refuse to be cut in on otherwise. The man who relinquishes his partner may not immediately cut back on that couple, but may cut in as soon as the young lady is dancing with someone else.

The modern tendency is for a young woman to dance all evening with her escort. Even when a group makes up a table for ten at a dinner dance it is not unusual for each man to dance only with his partner of the evening. Obviously this is an especially poor arrangement. Young people thus become accustomed to dancing with the same partner. A girl can follow her beau's lead but is like a beginner on the rare occasions when she dances with another man. For this reason hostesses, dance committees and floor committees try ways to break up this pattern. One method is the "double cut," in which two couples change partners. This is possibly the easiest and most satisfactory way to insure a temporary change. Another, which is the responsibility of the floor committee, is to see that the stag line is active—i.e. that the men who have no dates with them cut in on girls whom they know. At big dances there is a tendency for the "unattached" men to talk among themselves, watch the festivities but take no active part in them. Obviously this is unfair to the hostess, the committee and the women at the dance.

Since "dance cards" or "programs" are now completely obsolete (and who regrets their passing?) and the modern trend to dance only with one's escort has about run its course, let's hope that the practical "open choice" dancing will soon return to favor. Until then stags must be encouraged to "cut in" and sensible couples will, at least occasionally, "double cut."

One "dance etiquette" rule that has not changed is that it is the lady who suggests leaving the floor. A gentleman may not do so, since this implies that he does not want to dance with her—an indirect snub. So, too, whether they are bumped by another couple, his partner steps on or kicks him, or he really does step on her foot, the gentleman is the one who apologizes, thus implying that her dancing is perfect and that if she walked on his foot it was in her way.

At a very large dance or public ball it is not possible for a man to ask the hostess or head of the committee to dance— unless he is in her own group. At a small dance it is courteous to ask her. So, too, at a small dance it is courteous to ask all in one's group or at one's table. Regardless of the size of the dance, the first dance of the evening should be with one's partner. It is bad manners for a girl to accept an invitation to dance with another man while her escort is checking his coat, bad manners for a man to sit through dinner or several rounds of drinks and then, ignoring his "girl" or wife, ask another woman at the table to dance with him.

If there are separate checking facilities, the young woman leaves her own tip. A married woman may ask her husband for the money to tip the attendant or for change to give the matron in the ladies room. A single girl should be sure to have sufficient change with her.

In recent years the business organization or professional group dinner-dance has produced a few special protocol problems. No matter how big the dance, some man in the organization should have the responsibility of getting that company's group together. Senior executives and their wives are tacitly the "guests of honor" for that group. In arranging the seating the junior executive or his wife must bear that in mind. Those seated at the table with guests of honor may not, under ordinary circumstances, leave before them. (If the purpose of putting them at the same table is to have a congenial group, why will wives insist on sitting next to their husbands?) Regardless of what others at their own tables do, men at the "organization's table" should ask the women to dance. Mr. Young dances first with his wife, then asks the wife of the board chairman for a dance, then asks the wife of the secretary, and so on. Since the present business trend is to evaluate both the up-and-coming man *and* his wife, Mrs. Young should be polite, sufficiently friendly and not too quick to offer her views on the firm's business, national politics or any controversial subjects. Let's hope that by the end of the evening, Mr. Powers decides that "that charming girl certainly is an asset to Jack Young." If she is overopinionated, loud or drinks too much she may be lucky to be classified only as "Jack's liability."

15

Hostess and Guest

WEEKEND VISITING IS one of the many English customs that we follow. Originally weekending was mostly confined to the summer months and to visits to the country, beach or mountain resorts. (The old joke about the country relatives only hearing from their city cousins in summer was often far too true.) Nowadays, however, weekend visits are popular at all seasons, and the residents of a city apartment are as likely to have weekend visitors as are the owners of a split level in the suburbs or a Cape Cod cottage at the shore.

It shouldn't be necessary to tell *anyone* in this day of telephones and easy communication that it is bad manners to go uninvited and almost worse to "invite oneself." Many otherwise well-bred people, who wouldn't think of dropping in on friends, don't seem to realize that the homeowner is the one who suggests a weekend visit—not, as they seem to think, the would-be visitor!

In extending an invitation for an overnight visit, it is correct to be definite. The hostess sets the day and time of arrival and of departure. How different this is from the days of our forefathers! Then Aunt Jane was invited to come for Thanksgiving, and if she so chose, she remained until after Christmas! Now we may say "Come on the five-thirty Friday evening. We'll meet the train at the junction. You can go back on Monday morning with Bob. He takes the nine-five." The invitation may be just as informal and direct as that. It may be either telephoned or written. Of course, if you have special plans for the weekend, explain them. If the guest will need a dinner dress or sailing gear, say so.

One of the etiquette rules that has not changed is also one that many modern young people completely ignore: a girl never accepts a man's invitation to visit his home, even though he lives with his family or is going home for the weekend and wants her to join him. Correctly, he finds out if she can go, then his mother or another woman member of the family writes or telephones and "seconds" the invitation. Today, in seven out of ten cases, a young woman has to *ask* the man to have some woman member of his family ask her. Yet I cannot imagine any situation more embarrassing than walking into the home of a woman whom you have never met and standing there while her son introduces you and adds, "I told Nancy you would love to have her come down with me."

Younger members of the family—this includes all unmarried sons and daughters—should "clear it" with their parents before inviting friends. This is not a case of obtaining permission. Rather it is a common-sense approach to what could turn into an embarrassing situation—if the parents expected guests and two or three of their offspring invited friends of their own. After all, few of us have unlimited guest rooms.

The ideal guest is the one who arrives when expected and brings all that she will need for her visit, including her own tennis racket, golf clubs, bathing suit and bedroom slippers! She does not, however, arrive with bulky or untidy luggage.

It is customary for an overnight guest to take a gift to the hostess. A man guest usually limits his selection to flowers, candy, a book or record (if he knows the family taste along these lines). A woman has a wide selection from which to choose. Her gift may be one of these or perfume, some personal articles or a small household gift. Naturally, if there are children in the home, a wise guest takes each one some small toy or trinket.

One of the first things for the guest to ascertain is the breakfast hour and family customs pertaining to it. Unless in homes of great wealth, it is customary for the family to have breakfast in dining room, breakfast room or kitchen. Nine out of ten families eat in the dining room when guests are present. Once in a while, however, a hostess actually prefers to have a guest breakfast in her room. In this case, the guest may be asked when she wants her tray. Obviously, in a small informal home in which there is no maid, the guest would prefer to be treated as one of the family. She may say she would like to join the family in the kitchen, but she can't persist if her suggestion is not accepted. Incidentally, the guest in a servantless home should offer to help with household chores, clearing the table, putting things away. Although some hostesses welcome this assistance, many prefer that the guest stay out of the kitchen. Here again, one may offer, but not insist. The guest in such a home, however, should keep the guest room clean, make the bed, empty guest-room ash trays, wipe the tub after using it and, in general, make as little extra work as possible. Naturally, in a home in which the guest uses the family bathroom, the guest does not hang nylons in the bathroom and makes a point of leaving it in order after she uses it.

I honestly don't think there's a printed breakfast menu available in any home today, with the possible exception of some fabulous mansion when a big house party is in progress. In the average maidless or one-maid home the hostess usually tells an overnight guest what the family has for breakfast and asks what the guest would like, possibly making some suggestions.

When a guest enters the dining room or family room for breakfast, she should be completely dressed—no hair curlers, no rollers, a dress or suit in the city; a dress or sport attire in the country.

The considerate guest does not take up all the hostess' time but finds some ways to amuse herself or keep occupied in her room or, at least, away from the family for a part of each day. After all, no matter how well they like the visitor, any family wants a bit of privacy once in a while. On the other hand, the guest who has friends in the vicinity should not make the mistake of rushing over there at every possible moment, making plans with these friends or accepting outside invitations without first consulting the hostess. (It can be very annoying if the hostess discovers that her house guest has a date for dinner and the movies on the night that she had planned a dinner party at the club for her.)

Partly because of the shortage of domestic help, partly because of the informal way in which most of us live, few houses today have sufficient servants to unpack guests' bags, lay out their night clothes and so on. If there are servants, the guest should only ask them to do for her as little as possible. For this reason, she sees that her wardrobe is in perfect order when she arrives, she takes with her clothes that require a minimum of care and if possible no pressing.

Whether or not the household servants do any personal chores for a guest, on departing the guest gives monetary gifts to those she has seen and, if she has been present for several meals, sends or takes to the kitchen a gift for the cook. She never asks the hostess to distribute such gifts for her, nor does she ever mention the gifts to the hostess.

The guest who hopes to be invited back never takes sides in a family dispute, does not argue religion or politics with host or other guests, does not overuse the telephone (either for outgoing or incoming calls), does not borrow the host's car or golf clubs, does not flirt with the host or with the daughter's beau, and says she slept well even if the dog's barking kept her awake, the bed was hard or there were too few blankets.

It is almost impossible to suggest clothes for a weekend or longer visit since what will be needed must depend upon the social activities of the hostess, the community, time of year, weather, what activities have been planned and what clothes the guest actually has. Obviously the guest in a big home in a social resort will do well to take along appropriate evening or formal clothes for the season. One who is invited to a friend's cabin in the woods will want clothes for roughing it, sturdy shoes, possibly one dress or semi-formal outfit for a country club dance.

The wise guest never extends the visit even if urged to do so. (Wasn't it George M. Cohan who said "Always leave them asking for more?") It is so much better to leave as planned than to allow oneself to be persuaded to stay longer —or, even worse, *suggest* staying another day.

Almost as bad as the guest who overstays is the one who leaves something after him. The things that guests forget to pack are truly amazing. Hostesses have found everything from a lipstick to a fur coat left in a guest room. A considerate guest does not leave film to be developed, clothes at the cleaners, or shoes at the cobbler when he leaves. It is disconcerting for a hostess to be asked "Will you please pick up my pictures at the druggist? I left a roll of film there yesterday." Or "When you have a chance, please get my coat that I left in the cleaners in town. He said it will be ready in a week. I've paid for it." This is not exaggerated. Many a hostess dreads the responsibility, to say nothing of the trouble involved, for picking up a guest's belongings and sending them to her.

If, on arrival, the guest did not have a gift for the hostess, one should be sent after the visit. But even more important than the hostess' gift is the bread-and-butter letter (thank-you note) that should be sent as soon as possible.

I'm convinced there is an art to being a good hostess. The type or size of the home does not enter into it, the abundance or lack of money has not too great a bearing on it. Certainly many a guest has spent a delightful weekend in the home of a "Mrs. Littlecoin" and a very dreary one in "Mrs. Greatwealth's" lavish abode. What makes a truly gracious hostess? An interest in people, the desire to have others enjoy themselves and, possibly most important, the ability to apparently enjoy her own party.

Most writers suggest that the hostess should put her guests at their ease. This is fine. My experience has been, however, that many visitors don't need to be "put at ease." Too many of them assume that, as guests, they have the run of the house. Certainly this is true about a great many visiting relatives.

We must bear in mind, however, that the hostess has definite obligations to her guests. Of these, possibly the most important is that she be at home when the guest arrives. I admit that this is sometimes difficult, especially if the guest travels by car. But if the guest has been told to "come Friday afternoon," the hostess should be at home all afternoon. Obviously the guest who comes by public conveyance of any kind—whether interstate bus, train, boat or plane—should be met by the hostess or some member of the family.

In social circles, it is permissible to have a chauffeur meet an arriving guest who is either a member of the family or a frequent visitor. It is not considered gracious for an employee alone to meet guests who are making their first visit.

Although it is not necessary to plan every minute of a house guest's stay, it is also not advisable to leave the guest to her own resources for long periods of time. On the other hand, the guest should be permitted free choice. It is possible that she does not share the hostess's interest in tennis and declines to go watch the junior matches at the club. This does not mean the hostess must also stay home. If she wants to sit on the porch and read a book, she'll like it better if it is not made clear that, since she won't go to the club, her hostess must change her plans.

The considerate hostess does not try to make over a guest, does not suggest how her hair should be worn or how she should dress. She doesn't expect guests to share her liking for pets or modern music or opera. If the guest happens to enjoy what her hostess enjoys—fine! Possibly she was invited because of their common interests. However, if a visit proves that they have little in common, neither should show disappointment. Above all, a hostess should not ask a guest to take sides in a family dispute or give an opinion about anything pertaining to family issues.

The hostess may not accept invitations while she has a house guest unless, after explaining the situation, she is told to "bring your guest (or guests) along." Years ago it was considered permissible for a hostess to keep her dinner date provided she made arrangements for the guest's amusement. This might occasionally be done nowadays in the homes of the fabulously rich, where guests are made to feel that they are in a very luxurious and exclusive hotel but where hostess and guest feel free to make their own plans, go their separate ways. This being so, however, why bother to issue the invitation for a visit?

Two things frequently puzzle an inexperienced hostess: is it proper to take the money for a long-distance phone call made by a guest, and is it proper to ask a house guest if she wants to go to church on Sunday?

If the amount is trifling—I'd say if it is under a dollar— the hostess should decline if it is offered. There is no reason why she should not accept the money for a really costly call. The guest who calls the Coast or Europe will feel much better about it if her hostess takes the money for it.

It is always correct to ask a guest if she wants to go to church. This does not mean just the church the hostess attends. The guest may say "I would like to go to mass at nine o'clock" or "What time could I conveniently go to mass?" If the hostess always attends church services and the guest does not want to do so, she should be allowed to stay home, not urged to go with the family.

Nowadays few men take unexpected guests home to dinner. However, there are times when this, according to the men, can't be avoided. In this case the "reluctant hostess" smiles sweetly. Let's hope that her larder can accommodate the additional person. If not, there is no choice—the couple should take the guest out to dinner. No matter how annoyed a hostess is about this sort of thing, she does not show it. Someone has said that unexpected guests account for many pairs of dark glasses. The hostess doesn't want to show the fire in her eyes!

The guest room should not be a catch-all for discarded furniture or worn linens. There should be a choice of one hard, one soft pillow, sufficient blankets for the time of year, and an extra one—in case the weather turns cool. The guest room closet should be empty of clothes and have sufficient hangers. The bureau drawers should also be empty and lined. If the guest must share the family bathroom, bath, hand and face towels and wash cloths, as well as facial tissues, should be left in the guest room. If possible, an emergency razor, toothbrush, toothpaste and cleansing cream should be either in the guest room or on a designated shelf in the bathroom.

Naturally it is pleasant if there is a TV set in the guest room; if, as is usually the case, this is not possible, a radio is an asset. A book or two and a current magazine are sure to be appreciated, also. But do be sure that it is a recent magazine!

In planning a house party, the hostess must be careful to have congenial guests. This does not mean that they must be in the same age group or have the same profession. It means that it is difficult to have an elderly man who dislikes music at the same party as two or three opera buffs or guitar players.

Weekend guests usually arrive in late afternoon or before dinner on Friday. Cocktails or tea should be available as soon as they have unpacked, freshened up and joined the group. Those who are new to the others should be introduced and guests should be given an outline of the next day's activities or possibilities.

At a large party it is permissible to ask guests you know well to share a room. Don't, however, make this suggestion to one who is a guest in the house for the first time. For instance, when a group of sorority sisters are overnight guests, the chances are they would prefer to double up, but two older women who have just met will hardly appreciate the suggestion that they do so.

The hostess who has no guest room but contrives extra sleeping arrangements with a "convertible" or a studio couch should, if possible, have a member of the family give up a bedroom to the guest and use the makeshift arrangements. This is especially important if in a small apartment the family has to pass through the room in which the temporary bed is set up. If there is no way to avoid putting the guest in the living room, at least a section of a closet, possibly a bureau drawer should be put at the guest's disposal. "Living out of a suitcase" is hardly conducive to a pleasant visit.

If there is a large house party, wedding, graduation or other special event that overflows the house, the host pays for rooms in hotel or club for some of the guests.

So much advice is aimed at the hostess and the woman guest. Actually, the "guest suggestions" apply to both men and women. Although most of the information applies to the hostess, some part of the responsibility for a pleasant weekend depends on the host. For one thing, he pays the bills— not merely the "hidden costs" of an extra in the household but the actual costs of any outside entertaining involved. Like the hostess, he puts up with petty inconveniences; like the hostess he smiles and does not show annoyance. At least, if he has to take guests sight-seeing, he has a chance to become acquainted with his community. He pays guest fees and food and bar bills at the country club, but such things as individual greens fees, special fees for the use of tennis courts, caddy tips and coach or "pro" charges are the responsibility of the guest.

The guest always pays his own traveling expenses and in the city pays for a taxi to take him to his destination. As I have said, in the country or suburbs he is met at the station.

A woman guest who so wishes may ask the hostess to be her guest at lunch or tea in some special restaurant or hotel the guest wants to see. This is quite correct, and the guest pays all the expenses involved. A woman guest, however, should not take the host and hostess out unless she can arrange to prepay the bill or have it charged to her (as in a club of which she is a member), since it would embarrass her host to have to sit at the table while a lady settled the bill.

Unfortunately, there are always hostesses who take advantage of visiting professionals. The pianist who is invited for the weekend is entitled to his free time. It is inconsiderate for a hostess to invite him, then use him as a drawing card to get other guests. So, too, it is bad manners to ask a professional artist to perform for other guests. The hostess who invites talented people to her home because they are a source of free entertainment for her and her other guests is guilty of the worst form of social snobbery. She is taking advantage of friendship.

One of the etiquette points that sometimes puzzle guest and hostess alike is "Who suggests retiring or ending the evening?" The guest who has her own room should retire to it at a reasonable hour unless there is some special reason to remain in the living or family room. On the other hand, if she likes to watch TV late at night, she may ask her hostess if it is all right for her to stay in the living room a while and put out the lights when she goes to her room. In this way, the hostess feels free to go to her room whenever she wishes. If the guest has to sleep in a family or living room, the hostess (all the family, actually) should make a point of retiring early, since she must otherwise wait politely until they leave her for the night.

16

*Social and
Business Correspondence*

TELEGRAMS, CABLES AND especially the telephone have certainly spared us lengthy letter writing many times over. The rapid pace of our lives today makes it seem impossible to get along without the time- and effort-savers. But there are occasions when it is imperative that we write a letter. And it is at those times that we envy our forefathers the ease with which they could compose and write a letter about almost any subject.

There are some people who actually like to write letters—but they are few and far between. Most of us really hate to sit down and write. If we are smart, we train ourselves to write all letters promptly—but, alas, too many of us say "I'll write tomorrow."

Business letters of any kind should be as short as possible, and to the point. The recipient may not want to spare the time to read lengthy ones. We should say what we have to say in as few words as possible. This does not mean that one need be blunt or curt. The phraseology can be polite and still brief. Social letters may obviously be longer, unless they are strictly formal.

Letters should be neat, with no blots or stains and no scratching out of words. Our handwriting may not be perfect but we should try to make it legible. Those whose writing is poor because of trying to write too rapidly should slow down. One who can't write a straight line should place a paper ruler or the edge of another piece of paper a trifle below each line as it is written or, if the paper is thin, put a piece of heavily ruled paper beneath and use these lines as a guide. Any of these methods should help to keep lines straight.

In our grandmother's day it was considered very bad manners to type a social letter. In our day of haste, of careless and often illegible writing I feel that common sense should be the guide here. A long letter home, a letter to an intimate friend, a chatty note to a relative—all these may well be typed. A letter of sympathy, a thank-you note to one much older or more important, a formal reply to an invitation— all these should be handwritten.

Possibly one of the most important things to say about letters is—don't read a letter not addressed to you! This means that a mother should not read her daughter's mail or, holding the envelope to the light, try to make out the signature of the writer. It means that the wife who thinks her husband is getting mail from a blonde should not try to intercept it. If the correspondence seems to be getting out of hand, she would do better to see her lawyer.

At present, double sheets of stationery are considered more formal but also more old-fashioned than single ones. Correctly one should write only on one side of a single sheet, but here again common sense must prevail. When double or "book" style paper is used, one writes on the first, third, then second and finally the back of the paper. The reason for going from the first to the third page is in order to follow the rule of not writing on the back of a page unless it is absolutely necessary. A two-page letter should therefore be on the first and third pages. It is not considered good form to number the pages of a letter. However, a long and complicated letter to a close friend might be more easily read if numbered—another time for the use of common sense.

Nowadays we have a far greater selection of paper than was available when letter writing was a necessity. However, for formal mail, it is usual to follow established custom. The average woman needs the following stationery: for all general social mail, single sheets, about 7 3/4 by 5 3/4 inches, preferably with monogram or initials in upper left corner; small double sheets, which may open up, rather than over. These are "informals" and are about 5 inches wide by 4 inches high, if opening up, or no more than 5 1/2 inches high by 4 wide if opening like a book. These informals usually have a small monogram in the upper left corner or a large monogram or the full name, as "Mrs. John Henry Smith," in the center. These may be used for thank-you notes, some third-person replies, enclosures with gifts. The woman who has a great deal of semi-business correspondence may also have single sheets about 8 by 5 1/2 inches, with the address only, centered at the top of the page. (Such stationery has an added advantage. Since it has no initials, all ladies of the family may use it.) The average man's stationery is the club size and may have his address at the top center. If he has a family crest, he may have it engraved at the top left of the paper with the address centered and dropped a little below. Occasionally men have a slightly smaller size for thank-you notes and so on, but most men prefer to use the club size for all social and semi-business correspondence.

Since so much of our mail nowadays is likely to be sent by air, thinner paper is more fashionable than formerly. Of course, it is possible to have heavy vellum paper for general use and special "air mail" sheets, but not many bother to have two weights of paper just for this reason. Conservatively lined envelopes are always permissible but not as fashionable now as they once were. So, too, pastel stationery, although acceptable, is not in best taste, and most conservatives confine themselves to white, off-white, pale gray and very pale blue. Men, of course, use white, off-white or gray paper.

Although mourning stationery is obtainable it is very seldom used at present. Plain white paper is usually preferred.

If paper is not engraved or printed, the address and date may be written at the top right side, about one to two inches from top of paper. The date alone is put at the bottom of page, left side when the address is printed at the top. This is always correct and conservative. At present, however, there is a tendency to put both address and date at bottom left when no address is printed at the top.

The salutation of a letter should always start with "Dear . . . ," which may be "Dear Mr. Brown" or "Dear Jane" or (for business, with full address above) "Dear Sir." The salutation to a clergyman is "Dear Father. . . ," "Dear Rabbi . . . ," "Dear Doctor. . ." or "Dear Mr. . . ." If he is referred to as "Pastor Brown," this is the proper salutation, but "Reverend Brown" is not used. The title "Doctor" is always written out in a salutation, although abbreviated in the address.

A formal letter or a formal invitation should be written all on one page. In the case of "double paper" this means on the first page. It is impossible to give rules about the length of other letters. Remember, however, that a change of subject calls for a new paragraph.

"Sincerely" or "Sincerely yours" are still the favored closings for social letters. "Yours truly" and "Very truly yours" are used for some semi-business mail. Affectionate closings should be confined to relatives and truly intimate friends. A girl or boy should not, as is currently the fad, close a letter to a casual acquaintance of the opposite sex "love" or "with love."

Mail sent to employees, including servants, should have the standard salutation. If the employee is referred to as "Miss Smith" at work, the salutation is "Dear Miss Smith" and if she is "Jane," the salutation is "Dear Jane." So, too, the closing should be either "Sincerely" or "Very truly yours" depending on the contents of the letter and your usual contacts with her.

Titles are never used in business signatures! A man simply signs "John Smith" and may add "M.D." or "D.D.S." A woman signs "Jane Smith," and adds below "(Mrs. John Smith)" if she is married. Without this addition, we assume that she is "*Miss* Jane Smith." Naturally this second line is never added to a social letter to a friend, nor does a doctor add his degree after his name in social correspondence. It is, however, advisable to sign the complete name when writing to all but intimates. A casual letter signed, "Jack" may puzzle the recipient if he knows several "Jacks."

Never address an envelope without giving a title, as "Mr. John Smith." If you don't know if she is married, address the envelope "Miss Jane Smith." If you know she is married and don't know her husband's first name, try to ascertain it as it is bad form indeed to address a letter "*Mrs.* Jane Smith." A widow or divorcee is still "Mrs. John Brown," *not* "Mrs. Mary Brown." A divorcee who resumes the use of her maiden name is "Miss Maiden Name," never "*Mrs.* Maiden Name." If she wants to be known as "Mrs." she should retain her married name. A doctor's wife is addressed as "Mrs. John Smith." I cannot understand why, in some sections of the country, she is called, "Mrs. *Dr.* John Smith"! A letter to a little girl, no matter how young, is "Miss Jane Doe." A small boy's mail is addressed "Master." He used to be so called until he was over sixteen, when he graduated to "Mr.," but now we start addressing his mail "Mr. John Brown" when he is ten or twelve. (Little boys grow up too fast and it sounds "quaint" to call a little-leaguer "Master.")

A letter of sympathy on a death should be handwritten. Printed cards do not suffice. If one is used, a few hand-written words should be added to give the note a personal touch. Telegrams of sympathy are also acceptable. The condolences are addressed to the member of the family the writer knows best or, knowing only the deceased, the "next of kin." Letters of sympathy should be brief, as

We were saddened to learn of Jack's death. All who knew him admired him and his work.

Words are rather futile, but we want you to know we are sorry.

The family of the deceased should write personal letters of appreciation to those who sent flowers, mass or other religious offerings, made donations to charitable funds in the name of the deceased, or wrote personal letters of sympathy. Printed sympathy cards do not need to be acknowledged. It is not necessary for the members of the family personally to write every letter, but the letters should go out in the name of the nearest or other close relative. If printed cards are used for this purpose, they should have space in which a short personal message may be written, such as mention of the flowers or the spiritual or charitable offering.

Sympathy letters to those who are ill can be gay and light. This is one of the times when printed cards are almost better than written notes. Obviously the "get well card" should be appropriate.

Never send a letter of introduction for one you do not honestly know. If you can truthfully do so, by all means write a letter. If to a friend, make it friendly and informal. To others or to a business organization, club and so on be direct, brief and to the point.

The letter that we are most careless about is the one that should be promptly written—the thank-you letter. Today it almost seems as if too many of us resent the suggestion that "thanks" are in order for gifts, visits, help in obtaining a job, and the like. Well-bred folk, however, always send gracious notes of appreciation when thanks are due. The rule to remember here is that we use the expression "thank you" and mention the gift, some high point of the visit, or, in the case of a job interview or a club application, tell the results to date. The engaged girl makes a point of mentioning her fiance's name in her thank-you letter for a wedding present, although she never makes the letter a "joint one."

A letter of congratulations is always a pleasant one to send. This is, of course, not obligatory, but it is a way to keep friends and is usually appreciated by the recipient. If there is not time for a letter (which can be more personal) telegrams may substitute.

Never write a letter of recommendation unless you sincerely mean it, and *don't* write a letter, then phone and say what you really think. The one who receives your letter and phone call will see through your deceit and dislike you for it. If you can't honestly endorse the job-seeker, the tone of your letter, although not saying anything damaging, will convey your apathy. (Of course, ideally one should decline to write a letter, but this is not always feasible.)

Formal invitations and replies are always in the third person. A hostess who gives a great many formal or elaborate parties may have engraved invitations and merely fill in names, dates and so on. If not, the invitation should be handwritten in ink. (I think that one who does not have need for engraved invitations should strive to make all her entertaining "semi-informal," which is far more fashionable today, and thus eliminates the third-person invitation.)

In writing an invitation for a dinner or reception in honor of someone the usual wording, on a large visiting card or an informal is, "To meet Dr. and Mrs. Henry Smith" with the date, time and place in the lower left corner. Not many formal teas are given nowadays, but if planned it is sufficient to simply put "Tea" and date and, if necessary, the place on either the engraved third-person invitation card or on a large-size visiting card. Cocktail parties are never really formal and therefore an informal invitation is the usual choice.

The bride who does not have many friends and relatives may write a handwritten invitation to those she wants to attend her wedding or may, if she prefers, send handwritten letters after the ceremony to let her relatives know of her marriage. Such letters are in social-letter form, not worded like either invitations or announcements. They are just as correct as engraved third-person ones.

In our grandparents' day it was not considered good form to put "R.s.v.p." in letter or invitation, since this implied that the writer doubted the recipient's manners. Nowadays we have become so indifferent, even callous about such things that young people will argue "If she wanted a reply, why didn't she make that clear!" For this reason I've given in and now advise anyone who wants and expects replies to fall back on the standard "R.s.v.p." I might add, however, that "reply cards and stamped envelopes" are never included in social invitations. These may be used for business or professional gatherings only. One's friends should be willing to reply without these inducements!

Although formal invitations must be answered in the third person, informal ones may be answered in whatever way is most convenient—note, telephone call or telegram.

Really personal messages should not be written on post cards. Cards to one's family may have only the first name. Others should have both first and last name. This rule applies to holiday greeting cards as well as scenic cards. Just as titles are not used in signing letters, they are not used in printed or engraved signatures on holiday cards. The only exception is when a third-person (formal) holiday message is used, as "Mr. and Mrs. John Smith wish you a very Merry Christmas and Happy New Year."

A social invitation to dinner nowadays gives the time guests are expected, which is in time for cocktails, although this is not mentioned. An invitation to a business or professional dinner or dinner-dance, however, states "Cocktail 7, Dinner 8" so that guests who wish may arrive just before dinner.

The one area of correspondence that more than any other can have long-range effect on the writer and her family is that of the combination business-social letter, invitation or acceptance. As we have noted of other phases of social usage, it is no longer true that our business and social worlds do not mix. On the contrary, in many cases they seem to merge. Certainly this is true of much of our present-day letter writing.

Some aspects of this correspondence that is "on the surface" social but with undertones of business are simple and easy to handle. We receive an invitation to the wedding of the board chairman's daughter. If, as is most often the case, it is an invitation to the ceremony and reception, we have no problem. We send back a formal (third person) acceptance. We mark the date on our engagement pad or calendar, and well in advance of the wedding we send a wedding present. A complication arises, however, when the invitation is to the church only. Should this be acknowledged? This answer is, of course, "no." However, this brings up the question, "Is a gift in order?" The answer here is qualified. It is true that an invitation to the church does not require a gift. But a certain amount of self-serving enters in. Does the boss expect or hope we'll send a gift? Would a gift be out of place, and so on. If the junior executive and his wife have met the prospective bride they may, without seeming to be trying to "curry favor," send a gift. If they have never met the bride but have taken part in social (business-social) activities with her parents a small gift and a friendly note are permissible. As with other aspects of business-social relationships, it is never wise to be too ready to establish or to emphasize the social side of the acquaintance. On the other hand, the ranking member of the firm has done this when he includes the junior executive in his guest list.

One of the most difficult letters to write and one about which an element of uncertainty is almost inevitable is the thank-you letter to an unseen host. Yet more and more this problem confronts those on the lower rungs of the executive ladder. Mr. and Mrs. Junior Executive are invited to attend a dinner or benefit of some kind, occupying the seats purchased by the firm or the company president. If, as is often the case, the president or ranking executive and his wife are present, they are the official host and hostess and a verbal expression of enjoyment, a polite "thank you for including us" on departure is sufficient. The situation is a little different, however, when the younger or junior couple find they are the sole representatives of the organization there. Is a thank-you letter in order? This depends on the manner in which the invitation was extended. If it was sent through office mail and addressed to the man or if the boss stopped by the junior's office or mentioned it to him on the phone, a social thank-you note is not necessary. If the invitation was not mailed home and was not addressed "Mr. and Mrs." and especially if the board chairman's wife doesn't enter the picture in any way, the younger man's wife has no obligation here. He should, however, make a point of thanking his superior and, if there were business undertones involved, should tell him something of what took place.

If, as is sometimes the case, an executive gives his theater or opera tickets to an assistant, a thank-you note from the assistant's wife is in order. It is far more personal to give tickets he had purchased for his own use to "you and Claire" than to include their names in the list of those to be seated at the company's table at a charitable or convention dinner.

Sometimes the head of a reasonably large organization invites all or most or a selected group of his employees to his home or club for a day. This is sometimes a tradition—a clambake, a cookout or simply a general picnic, complete with baseball game, potato race, possibly swimming. Under such circumstances, what, in the way of thank-you letters, is expected of employees and the wives of those who are married?

Since it is assumed that those who are invited to spend the day at his home will not repay the obligation in kind, a short note of thanks from each employee is the gracious thing. On the other hand, the employees may correctly group together to send flowers with a brief "thank-you" enclosed or they may write a thank-you letter with all signatures or merely a group signature, as "The Administration Department." Such a note or expression of appreciation should be addressed to "Mr. and Mrs." and sent to the home address. Needless to say, if this type of socializing is confined to a very small group, while a note is a gracious gesture, it is expedient to reciprocate in some more personal, certainly more "social equal" way.

The kind of stationery that the rising young couple uses can do much to make or break them among the wives of the executive clan. It should be obvious that flashy paper, gaudy colors or decorations, vividly lined envelopes can by their lack of taste put the unfortunate husband at a disadvantage. There is, however, another side to the coin. A research chemist of my acquaintance was passed over for promotion because the wives of his superiors resented the heavy quality stationery with engraved family crest that his wife used for her social correspondence. The good ladies felt that she "gave herself airs" because her writing paper was so obviously correct and in good taste—but also very expensive. From the foregoing it should be apparent that, so far as social-business contacts are concerned, the wise wife selects her writing paper with care, avoiding tawdry motifs, gaudy or too conspicuous colors but also being careful to avoid paper that might mark her as too socially conscious or too ostentatious. Obviously she is careful and circumspect about what she puts into her letters. Since, in these contacts, she is striving, albeit unconsciously, to be a good will ambassador for her husband, she answers all invitations and writes all letters of thanks as promptly as possible.

17

Business Etiquette

BUSINESS AND SOCIAL etiquette have one thing in common. The basis of both is courtesy. Otherwise in many areas they are separate and distinct. Stop to think about it and this is entirely logical. It would be impossible to accomplish much in the average business organization if we indulged in the social amenities during working hours. On the other hand, courtesy and common sense always smooth our path in the business as well as the social world.

Early writers on etiquette painted a dim picture for the brave young women who, mostly through necessity, looked for work in the male-dominated world of business. They pointed out that a girl should not look for romance during working hours, that an office was not the hiding place of Cupid. Nonsense! Although most women still seek employment outside the home mainly for money, there is a rapidly enlarging corps of career girls who work for the very reason that they thus enlarge their acquaintance, meet interesting people, gain a broader horizon—and hope to find Prince Charming while doing so.

Whatever their reason for entering the competitive world of work, most women in the United States work before marriage—and a great many after marriage. They may "enjoy being a girl," but they should not try to "cash in" on their sex during business hours.

Whatever her job, wherever her field of endeavor, unless she is supplied with a uniform, a woman is expected to dress neatly and appropriately. The usual choice is a simple daytime dress or a softly tailored suit. Unless she's in a business that calls for extremes in dress or make-up, her watchword should be "conservative." Extreme hairdos, too much and too ornate jewelry, heavy perfume and plunging necklines are out of place in an office, behind a counter, or among the library bookshelves. One other hint for the distaff side—it is permissible to take a quick look in one's mirror and do minor retouching to make-up while at one's desk. Hair combing, applying mascara or lipstick, or a thorough powdering of the face calls for a trip to the ladies room. Even if your job doesn't bring you into contact with the public, your co-workers should not be "treated" to your excessive grooming while you are at your desk.

As I have said, it is quite possible to find romance in the office but in most cases this is the exception rather than the rule. The beginner in a business organization may well get attention from the young men who are her contemporaries. If they have about the same business status, there is no reason why a girl may not accept lunch invitations, even an occasional invitation to dinner and a show. Lunch invitations from an older man, possibly an executive, call for more serious consideration, however. And remember, the married members of the staff won't wear signs proclaiming this, nor do all married men wear wedding rings. There's one other angle from which to consider "office friendships," whether with a young clerk or a much older and quite important junior executive. The friendship may be fine while it lasts, but if it breaks up there may be resentment on the man's part or, if he turns his attention to a co-worker, the girl may find her situation embarrassing.

Having noted the disadvantages, the girl who decides to try mixing her business and social life should still be a bit circumspect about it. No matter how often she sees Mr. Jones outside the office, she should refrain from telling this to her co-workers, she should refrain from talking intimately to him in the presence of others. If he is "Mr. Jones" in the office, it is not smart to call him "Jack" when she addresses him in the presence of others.

There are, of course, occasions on which a married employer may need to have his secretary work overtime. In a lonely section this may necessitate sending out for dinner or going to dinner with the employer and returning to work. In such a case the employer should either give an employee taxi fare or, if convenient, drop her off on his way home. These "overtime work" sessions, however, should be on a strictly business basis, and the girl who is old enough to hold this type of job is old enough to know if the situation is getting out of hand.

In most cases the employer or the executives in an organization set the standard. The boss who is sufficiently considerate and courteous yet will not be imposed upon usually has the respect of those under him.

Since social manners are out of place in business, a man does not rise when a woman employee or co-worker enters his office or stops at his desk. He doesn't stand and draw up a chair for his secretary when she enters to take dictation.

He does, however, open a window or door that seems heavy for her, and obviously a gentleman would not remain seated while a woman employee struggled with a package, file case or any awkward or heavy object.

In some businesses such as banks, shops and other places where employees are in constant contact with the public, men wear jackets. In some, such as newspapers, advertising offices, behind-the-scenes in TV studios, engineering firms and so on, it is customary for the men to remove their jackets. Under such circumstances a man in his "shirt sleeves" need not put on his coat when a woman employee enters but would, of course, don it when he expected a woman caller— whether on a business or social visit.

There is one area in the average business building where men often seem unsure of what is correct—the elevator. Men don't step aside to let all women enter or get off the elevator first. This is not efficient, nor is it efficient for a man to remove his hat in a business elevator. However, if he is with women or meets feminine co-workers, he removes his hat if he conveniently can, and also if possible allows them to enter the elevator ahead of him. This is seldom possible when getting off because if they preceded him on he is nearer the door and it is therefore usually practical for him to get off first. The advent of the self-service elevator in business buildings sometimes causes uncertainty among the passengers. Does each one push the button for his floor or should one push his own, then ask what floors the others want indicated? If the elevator is open to the general public, each passenger pushes the button for his floor. If it is so crowded that some can't get near the button panel, it is usual to ask one near it to indicate the various floors.

The newcomer in an office is taken around by the office manager or someone assigned to the task and introduced to those with whom he'll come in contact. It is not necessary to introduce him to all in a large office, but he should meet those near him, those with whom he'll work, and those whose jobs relate to his own. The usual introduction is "Miss Brown— this is Jack Smith, the new mail boy." Jack is then told "Miss Brown has charge of sales promotion."

One who is new in an office does not make the first "friendly" advances. A new stenographer waits until another asks her to join her or a group for lunch. She may ask suggestions about restaurants, but she should not ask if she can have lunch with the others. She should avoid being "pushy" or too talkative and should refrain from giving her opinion, making comments about co-workers, and in other ways incurring the displeasure of those with whom she works.

In any place of business it is customary for the worker who enters at the start of the day to say "good morning" to those he passes. So, too, on leaving, he says "good night." Obviously, he doesn't make either his arrival or departure overly conspicuous, nor does he speak to one who is engrossed in work.

If the working hours are nine to five, an employee should be ready to work at nine o'clock. This does not mean "arrive at nine and take twenty minutes for make-up or to phone home." Remember, too, that a fifteen-minute coffee break should be confined to fifteen minutes. Don't stop work at four-thirty and spend a half hour preparing to leave, then rush to the doors at the stroke of five.

It is often difficult to avoid lateness in crowded business sections since traffic can delay bus or car. However, one who allows himself extra time for traveling can almost always arrive at his destination promptly or no more than a minute or two late. In keeping business appointments it is imperative that the caller arrive on time or notify the one with whom he has the appointment that he has been delayed. It is irritating for one who has to wait, whether in his office or elsewhere.

If an office door is closed, business courtesy requires that one knock. It is not necessary, however, to knock before entering if the door is open. In this case a subordinate hesitates inside the door until the occupant of the office notices his presence. A business contemporary or superior walks right in. If the door is closed, if it is known that a conference or confidential discussion is in progress, or there is a caller in the office, an employee should be sure that his reason for knocking is sufficiently important to warrant an interruption.

The telephone is an essential part of our business and social life. During working hours the phone is for business, and the employee who is permitted to make or receive personal calls should not abuse the privilege. Such calls should be as few and as brief as possible. Indeed it is possible and usually advisable to make business calls brief without being curt. One who takes a telephone message for a co-worker should write it and be sure to leave the note where it will be seen. (A message left on one's own desk won't mean much to a co-worker at the other end of the office.)

The executive who makes a phone call through a secretary or telephone operator should be ready to speak when the call is completed. It is annoying for the one called to be told "Hold the wire, please. Mr. Jones wishes to speak to you." If the phone rings while you are talking to someone at your desk, apologize for the interruption before you answer it.

A salesperson or anyone constantly in contact with the public has special business etiquette problems. Possibly one of the biggest mistakes a salesclerk makes is in trying to appraise a prospective buyer. The quiet little woman in black may be prepared to spend more than the flashy looking, self-assured one. A wise clerk does not "talk down" to customers, never implies that the customer can't afford the item she asks about. Above all, a clerk does not continue a trivial conversation when anyone is waiting for service. Despite the tendency to call total strangers "dearie," "darling" and "honey," such terms are bad manners and inexcusable in any shop.

The shopper must remember that others are entitled to the same service and courtesy as she. A considerate shopper does not try to get waited on out of turn, does not upset stock, idly pick up and handle merchandise, interrupt an obviously busy clerk or in other ways show a lack of consideration for others.

I'm convinced that our business manners, our attitudes toward the strangers we meet in a routine day are far more indicative of our true selves than our social manners. It is easy to be courteous to those we like and understand. The true test of a lady and gentleman is their attitude toward those who are not really important (except in passing) to them.

18

Sports and Clubs

EVEN FOR THOSE who are neither sports-minded nor club-minded, the etiquette of sportsmanship and clubmanship can be important. In normal social dealings—and perhaps even more in social-business dealings—you may sometimes find it impossible to decline an invitation to make a fourth at tennis or to refuse the Board Chairman's so well meant offer to put you up at his club during your business trip to San Francisco.

If you are the suburban wife of a young executive, you literally haven't a prayer of avoiding some involvement in sports. A fairly high percentage of your friends will be ardent (or apparently ardent) sportswomen, and a certain percentage of these will probably be the wives of your husband's business associates. It is, moreover, quite possible that your community may, by local tradition, recognize one or more sports as being socially "in." It may be yachting in Atlantic seaboard towns, tennis farther inland, golf, riding or whatever. But so large a degree of the community's social life—both during the week and on weekends—may be woven about these sports and the clubs that sustain them that non-participation can be a real handicap.

Participation. That is the key word . . . not necessarily a show of feverish enthusiasm or a display of great skill, but an amiable willingness to participate and a grace in the manner of doing so.

The first rule of sport is: Know the game. The important thing in a club is: Know the club rules.

Sportsmanship is no more than good manners applied to sporting activities. The man or woman who is truly well bred has little to learn of fundamental value that will improve his relations with his companions in swimming, tennis or other sports. A few superficial conventions that bear on any game are easily mastered when one understands that they are essentially practical, and that their observance makes for greater enjoyment all around.

I started to say: Don't take part in a game that you are not qualified to play, with players whose skill is too far beyond yours. But I'm inclined to think that the average person underestimates rather than overestimates his ability. So my advice is: Be perfectly frank about your skill in any sport. The girl who says "I can just manage to knock a ball around a court," and knows very well that she is considered a good player at home, is guilty of evasion. The man who insists that he can't swim more than a few feet, yet outdistances his companions, may not intend to show off, but he gives that impression. Needless to say, such an impression may be distinctly prejudicial.

In the world of sport no allowance is made for the weaker sex, and this is as it should be. The girl who starts out for a round of golf on a caddyless course should not expect a male player to carry her golf bag for her. When she hikes, hunts or rides, she accepts the unpleasant circumstances with the pleasant. There are the ordinary courtesies that a man extends—as when riding he keeps to the left of his companion in order to have a free right hand if her horse needs curbing —but a courtesy is not a burden imposed upon the one who extends it.

There are other courtesies that the well-bred person and sportsman should not need pointed out to him. A good swimmer does not "dare" an inexperienced one to attempt stunts. It is one thing to like the water yourself and take your fun boldly, but another to force your friends to your pace. Too many accidents are caused by this type of foolishness. Nor is there anything to be gained on a golf course when a group of slow players holds back a group of fast players. The fast players should be allowed to go ahead, and they should smile their thanks.

Let's sum up some of the fundamental dos and donts of the world of sports:

Know all the rules of the game. If you are not an expert player, explain this before joining an experienced group, but thereafter, avoid apologizing for your lack of skill while the game is in progress.

Accept the judge's decision whenever possible. If you honestly think there's an error, explain your stand quietly.

Learn to be a good loser. As a society, we think too much of winning. Adelaide A. Procter once said, "He who knows how to fail has won a crown whose lustre is not less."

Don't lose your temper when you're losing, which is simply the negative statement of: Learn to be a good loser. Or put it this way: Don't develop a headache when the game's going against you.

Don't make comments on your opponent's playing.

Don't give unsolicited advice.

Don't make excuses.

Don't talk too much.

Men have always had their gathering places in town where they could escape from family life. When the emancipation of women enabled them to engage their time lightly at games, they too were brought into the rosters of clubs, where they could make friends and entertain conveniently. These are the social clubs. There are clubs dedicated to other than social purposes: athletic, political and literary clubs, which spring from one need or another and can exist as often as not without a clubhouse. Country and beach clubs, on the other hand, have a combined function. Fundamentally social, they undoubtedly have their origin in a prevalent interest in outdoor sports. As a nation we are truly becoming addicted to club life.

There are various ways of joining a club, just as there are various reasons for joining. One way is to help found it. The usual way is through an acquaintance who is a member and proposes you. Occasionally it is possible to apply for membership.

The person who proposes another for membership in an organization should see that the "prospect" meets some of the officers or outstanding members; otherwise he has not fulfilled his obligation. Very often a lunch is arranged at which several of the board members meet prospective members. Or it is customary in many women's clubs to have special days when new members are presented to the board of governors. When this is the procedure, the member who proposes a friend should accompany the friend to the meeting.

I have said that it is important to know the club rules. It is equally important to obey them. If you wish to be liked in the group you have joined (and who doesn't?) you will conform faithfully to the practices of the group.

Many city clubs are so formal that members do not speak without an introduction. In other clubs, an older member may speak to one younger, but never a younger member to one older. There can be no fixed rules for conventions of this sort because they vary with the club.

The new member especially should avoid "pushing." It is not necessary to be a retiring, timid, colorless soul, but there is a difference between natural friendliness and aggressiveness that forces you on others. In entering the club dining room, don't rush over and join a group. If they want you to lunch with them they will ask you. In entering the card room, if you find a game of bridge in progress don't make comments or suggestions. You may decline to join the game if you are asked to do so, but don't express a dislike of the pastime. The last suggestion is not confined in its application to clubs. It can be applied every day, anywhere.

One should be as careful of the furnishings of a club as one is of the furnishings of a house. The person who is truly careful of a home will be. Never neglect your club dues, charges, card or other debts. If membership in a club becomes too great an expense, resign while in good standing. Don't wait until you are posted for non-payment.

Since the average man's club is considered a strictly masculine spot, a gentleman seated at the window of his club does not bow or speak to a lady of his acquaintance who passes. If the lady happens to see him, she tactfully does not appear to do so. In a club with a mixed membership, however, this ruling may be relaxed, and the lady may wave if she likes. But since it is always awkward to exchange greetings at that distance, it is just as well to establish the practice of never looking directly at the windows of clubs. City clubs, that is. This is a convention that does not obtain at country or suburban clubs.

The guest at a club is careful, first of all, never to impose. He should show the friend who is host the same courtesy he would give him in his own home. It would be rude to comment unfavorably on the service, decorations or club membership, and certainly no guest should assume proprietary airs.

The friend who "puts a guest up" at a club is not a host. The guest must not use his locker or cabana or personal property without specific permission.

The guest should tip those who give him special service: the locker steward at a beach club, the servant who makes up the room, the porter and so forth.

There is one outstanding difference between town and country clubs. A man joins a town club for himself alone, but when he joins a country club (with the possible exception of a shooting club) he wants his family and friends to share the club privileges.

Most country clubs are easier of access than town clubs, and it is often possible to obtain "season membership" privileges. This has obvious advantages for the family renting a summer place in the vicinity who would not be able to use the club the year round.

While country clubs are by their nature less formal than town clubs, they inevitably have their rulings—and it is the wise member who obeys. The lone wolf, the revolutionary, the iconoclast has no place in a social organization where people's likes and dislikes must be dovetailed into a neat pattern.

19

The Child

ACCORDING TO ANTHROPOLOGISTS, all human societies, from the most primitive to the most complex, observe what are called "rites of passage." These are celebrations of those periods in people's lives when they pass from one state to another—when they are born, when they come of age, when they marry and when they die.

The rituals by which society recognizes the mysterious importance of these changes in the life of every individual are basic to any code of etiquette. People are seldom more alive to the necessities of form and decorum than at these times.

It would be stretching a point to try to think of our participation in these rites primarily in terms of the effect on our own social positions or professional aspirations. With the possible exception of the coming-of-age ceremonies (much denatured in our contemporary society) these events are too basic, too personally significant to the people involved to warrant the intrusion of attitudes of self-interest. We all know, of course, that the possibility of giving offense through incorrect or unseemly behavior is at least as great at these times as at any other. We can imagine what the social or business consequences of such behavior could be. But having said this, let us set these considerations aside and return to more elementary and important matters.

In this and the succeeding eight chapters we shall discuss the etiquette that pertains to these "rites of passage" as they exist in our own society today. And since the beginning is a notoriously good place to begin, let us commence with birth and babies.

When a baby is born, his arrival is of great interest to family, relatives and close friends. Social custom demands that the birth should be announced as soon as possible. The immediate family, doting grandparents, aunts and uncles (on both sides) should be notified first. In fashionable circles in New York and other large cities, a notice is sent to the society editors of the newspapers. This is usually considered sufficient, since the close relatives have been told by telephone. In most parts of the country and among most big-city dwellers, the accepted custom is to send the parents' visiting card with a small card attached. The smaller card bears the new baby's name and the date of birth. The parents who do not have visiting cards should send the simplest card possible; in some cases this is a replica of a visiting card and has space for the parents' and baby's name and the birth date to be filled in. Comic birth announcements, cards that give the birth weight and so on are not in best taste.

The next traditional step is the christening or a formal bestowal of the baby's name. There is no set time, just as there is no set hour, for this. Roman Catholics usually baptize children within three or four weeks—preferably the former. Protestants on the other hand wait until the child is from six weeks to six months old. Some parents believe in a temporary name-bestowal and wait until the child is about sixteen years when he selects his own name. In this case, there is no ceremony or christening celebration.

A christening ceremony may take place in church or at home. In a church ceremony, the clergyman takes care of all necessary details. At home, however, the parents should see that all necessary equipment is available—a table with small white or lace cloth, at which the clergyman stands, a bowl, usually a pitcher, a small (guest) white towel.

Godparents are usually members of the family or intimate friends. In some communities it is customary to have the couple's honor attendant and best man at their wedding serve as godparents for the first baby. This is not an etiquette ruling, however, and is not a prerogative to be taken for granted even in communities where it is the usual practice. The Roman Catholic Church requires two sponsors at the christening—a godmother and a godfather. Some Protestant faiths have two of each, while others require two godmothers and one godfather for a girl, two godfathers and one god-mother for a boy.

In selecting a name (or names) for the baby, consider your family name and please give the child a name that will "go well" with it. In general, it is wise to avoid odd or un-usual names or one that may make the infant the butt of silly jokes when he is of school age. Some parents use the mother's or any family name as a middle name. Thus the child of John and Mary (Brown) Smith might be called John Brown Smith. This practice has a great deal to recom-mend it. It carries on family names and, in the case of rather plain or commonplace last names, it adds a definite individuality. Certainly "John Brown Smith" stands out

better than plain "John Smith" or "John Joseph Smith."
Family names are equally correct as middle names for girls,
but here's a word of caution about the selection of girls'
names: don't choose a "popular" name for a defenseless
child! "Kim" and "Shirley," "Karen" and "Ginger" may sound
cute while the baby is in her carriage. They'll be out of style
by the time she starts school and when she is an adult most
women meeting her will be able to guess her age within a
year or two, simply by recalling the period in which everyone called girl babies "Shirley" or the time when "Kim" was
the fad. If you must give the little girl a boy's name (and
elderly relatives, the possibility of her being remembered in
a will, and so on can be compelling reasons) please try to
make it a middle name. The feminine-looking teenager
named "George" or "Peter" has a great deal of explaining
to do.

The mother, godmother and other women relatives invited
to witness the christening or attend the reception that follows wear conservative afternoon dresses and, if the ceremony is in church, those who attend it wear hats. The godfather and father usually wear business suits, although in the
case of very social or prominent families they sometimes
wear morning coats and gray striped trousers.

Since most christenings take place while the baby is quite
young and the mother is still adjusting to the household addition, the reception is always limited to the immediate
families or very close relatives and friends. It is never a
"party" in the true sense of the word; rather it is a reception
or more or less formal tea. (Needless to say, "tea" is not
mandatory but the usual hours—from about three until five
in the afternoon—mean that a typical tea menu is in order.
Tiny sandwiches, small cakes, tea, champagne or standard
cocktail-hour drinks are served. Some people prefer to follow

tradition and serve a white iced cake (similar to a birthday cake) and caudle. The latter is a hot egg nog that was supposed to be good for the new mother and that she and others drank as a toast to the baby.)

All expenses pertaining to the child's christening—a stipend to the clergyman, any necessary fees to sexton or church—are the responsibility of the child's father. The godparents usually give "lasting" presents—a silver cup, porringer, or knife, fork and spoon set. A godparent may open a bank account for the child or buy the christening dress. In these practical days of very young parents on small budgets, it is not unusual for a godparent to give a baby carriage or even subscribe to a diaper service!

All invited to the christening buy gifts for the baby. Relatives and close friends not invited often do so, but this is far from obligatory.

Obviously the best way to teach a child manners is by example. It is never too early to start this form of teaching, for good manners acquired in babyhood are a natural part of the youngster as he grows up.

I don't for one minute mean that it is possible to teach table manners or neatness at an early age. But cheerfulness is a form of politeness and the child whose mother greets him with a cheery "good morning," who is calm and relaxed *part of the time* and who tries to show an interest in a tiny child's interest, is starting that child on the road to politeness and consideration for others.

In our grandparents' day it was usual for the average family to make a kind of formality of mealtimes. In the usual home, the children washed up before the evening meal, someone said grace and the little ones ate in silence, following the rule "Children should be seen and not heard." Such meals were ordeals in many ways, but the youngsters did acquire confidence at the table. On the other hand, more prosperous families banished the children to an early nursery or kitchen supper and they were not served at the family dinner table until they were young adults. Oh, no, they did not grow up with careless table habits, for a governess or their mother was on hand to give pointers on proper manners.

In our streamlined modern days we pride ourselves that the children are always with their parents, that they are often permitted to dominate the conversation. But there are serious drawbacks here, too. Many of us eat casual meals, TV dinners or sandwiches served in the living room, a soup and salad at the kitchen serving counter. This saves time and work for the homemaker, but it doesn't help the child to gain poise at a dinner table.

Once the child is able to feed himself, even if clumsily, he should be encouraged to do so. He should be taught the use of the napkin and each basic piece of silver. He should be taught to sit erect and to refrain from playing with the silver or napkin. He should be taught that neatness at table and the right way of eating are important, but he should not be scolded for accidentally spilling milk or dropping a piece of bread.

The average young mother tries to teach the small child the fine points of table manners during mealtimes. This is a mistake, and especially out of order if the youngster eats at the table with grownups. The constant correction, fussing and admonishing of children is irritating to adults at the table. Actually, children acquire their basic manners from their environment, from example. Too many of us, however, neglect to instill in our offspring consideration for others, respect for authority, and courtesy toward their elders. The small boy whose table manners are far from perfect will gradually improve them as he watches others eat. But the child who has never been told the importance of obedience, never been taught respect for teachers, parents and others in authority won't easily acquire this later. The one is a mechanical thing, the other is a part of personality. Mechanical habits are easy to correct, personality ones are more difficult.

School-age children should be taught to care for their books, toys and clothing. They should be helped in acquiring good grooming habits. When a child is old enough to write or print, he should be taught to write "thank you" notes to those who have sent him gifts, shown him some special consideration or in whose home he has been an overnight guest.

Confirmation and bar mitzvah, although religious services, are usually followed by receptions or parties of some kind. The child who receives confirmation is the guest of honor and it is usual for those invited to buy presents. A monetary gift is also correct and, for a child of this age, often a wise choice. The attire of the guest of honor, his parents and guests at the party must depend on the time it takes place and their usual custom. Those of the Jewish faith usually plan more elaborate festivities than do Christians. It is not unusual for the bar mitzvah to be followed by a seated dinner at which dinner jackets are correct for the men, simple dinner dresses for the women present. On the other hand, most confirmation parties are afternoon gatherings and business suits and afternoon dresses are the rule.

Although it is understandable that the children in the immediate family will be included, provided they are old enough, as a rule it is not advisable to have children at christening, confirmation, wedding and graduation parties. Parents of small children should not assume that a wedding invitation includes the whole family. They should not be insulted because their three little ones are not invited to a seated dinner following a bar mitzvah. It is well to remember that it is never permissible to take along the children unless specifically told to do so. And one final word of advice: the parents are responsible for their children throughout a party! It is unfair and inconsiderate for the father and mother to enjoy themselves while their restless or overtired youngsters snatch things from the buffet table, run around on the dance floor, or in other ways disturb the adult guests. If the parents want to practice "togetherness," they should do it all the way and keep their small children with or near them throughout the party.

20

Debutantes and Debuts

THERE ARE THOSE who hotly denounce the social custom of debutante parties, who insist that "coming out" has lost all significance because the girls who are introduced have been going to parties, having dates, often traveling alone for a year or two—sometimes more—before they are officially launched.

To me it seems strange that in a country where the "sweet sixteen party" (always in dubious taste) is becoming more and more popular there should be so much criticism of the girl who is presented to society two years later. My own feeling on the subject of debuts is that they have been commercialized, that far too many girls come out at big balls and have no true party of their own. In addition, as in other areas of our contact with youth today, there is too much laxity on the part of many of the parents who give parties for their daughters.

Originally the girl was kept in the social background until

she was eighteen, then was presumed to be mature enough to enter the social world of her parents and their friends— and ready to meet eligible young men. Well, what is the background of a "sweet sixteen" party? Actually, its purpose is the same. It simply launches the girl into her particular social group when she is younger than the average debutante.

In our grandmother's time, a debut was a dinner or ball given in the parents' home in honor of a daughter who had finished her schooling. Nowadays no well-bred girl has a debut until she finishes secondary school. But four out of five debutantes have not finished their education. They go on to college, junior college or some form of business training. This alone drastically changes the picture of the average debutante's year. Then she spent a whole year, or at least a season, going to lunches, dinners and dances. Being a debutante was a full-time job, and many mothers and daughters thought that the goal was to "get her man" before the season ended. Nowadays, despite the many very young brides, debutantes are no more concerned with getting a husband than the girls who, for one reason or another, don't "come out."

Since so many of the girls who will be presented and their logical escorts attend college, most of the debutante parties are held on weekends or during holidays. In New York, the Thanksgiving vacation period is crowded with such parties. Each year the Junior League Debutante Ball, the Grosvenor Ball, the Gotham Ball and the First Junior Assembly are held during this long weekend. Unlike the coming-out dances of years ago, the big balls are for worthy causes and the parents feel that in addition to presenting their darling daughter, they are also donating to a favorite charity. In the case of the Gotham, the Foundling Hospital is the beneficiary; Grosvenor House is helped by the ball that bears its name.

The girl who is really "in" in New York society usually is presented at or attends one or all of these Thanksgiving dances. At them she sees the girls and young men whom she has known most of her life. She has attended the same dancing classes, possibly gone to the same pediatrician and dentist as many of them. She has met them at the subscription parties that her group attended in their pre-debutante years.

In addition to being presented at one of the big balls, such a girl also has her own party. This may be a dinner or supper dance in a hotel or club. It may be a small dance at home or a dinner party preceding one of the dances. Sometimes a very conservative family has a reception for older friends of the family and, at another date, a tea dance for the debutante's own group.

If the girl has gone to the "right" schools, always mixed in the same group, has the right qualifications and five members endorse her, she may, with luck, be accepted as a provisional in the Junior League. Also with the right connections and sponsors, she may be accepted in the Colony Club.

With variations the same pattern is followed in other communities. There is the Salem Assembly for Massachusetts girls, the Bachelors' Cotillion in Baltimore, the Veiled Prophet Ball, the Terpsichorean Ball, Tuxedo Autumn Ball and many others.

In addition to these old-established social functions, however, there are many other subscription dances at which young women are presented and the proceeds from which go to charity or scholarship funds.

In small communities or those not near a big city, the debutante party is usually held in the girl's home, the country club or, in some instances, a community center. In this case the girl may have her own party or two or three sets of parents may combine and have a party for their daughters. But whether the debut is in New York's Hotel Plaza with Lester Lanin's orchestra or in the town community center with the high school trio providing the music, if a girl or girls are presented to their parents' friends and their own contemporaries it is a "debut" and the young woman is formally introduced in her own circle.

At debutante presentation dances there is a receiving line and the girls to be presented are introduced to those who are "receiving." If a girl has her own party, she and her mother greet their guests and, in the case of older friends, the mother presents the debutante, as "Mrs. Jones, my daughter Jane." Jane extends her gloved hand and says "How do you do, Mrs. Jones." Usually after an hour or so of greeting guests Jane is free to dance and enjoy the party.

Ideally, the guest list for a private party is made up of family and friends. In securing boys to serve as ushers or to fill the stag line the preferred plan is for the debutante's parents to invite sons and other young men relatives of their friends. The debutante can usually suggest names of boys she has met at other parties, the brothers of her classmates, and so on. Nowadays each girl invited to a subscription dance brings two escorts. When invited to a private party, she usually has only one. In either case, it is customary for the girls to send the names of their escorts to their hostess or the ball committee.

It is, of course, possible to have a social bureau take over the planning of a debutante party, and in this case it is usual for the bureau to supply extra boys—usually from a list of students in Ivy League colleges. In some communities, it is possible to obtain such a list on payment of a fee. I'm sure many of these young men are worthwhile, but I would not want to give a party and not really know my guests, and in the case of a young girl's party this seems doubly important.

A big subscription dance for debutantes is always called a ball, cotillion or assembly. On the other hand, no matter how big the party, a private dance is referred to as a "dinner dance," "supper dance" or "a small dance." The latter is the most popular term at present. Invitations to such a private party are usually engraved cards, sometimes the standard formal invitation that may be obtained in any good jewelry shop or stationers, more often especially engraved for the occasion. The typical wording follows:

> *Mr. and Mrs. John Henry Doe*
> *request the pleasure of*
> *(name is filled in in ink)*
> *company at dinner in honour of their daughter*
> *Miss Jane Doe*
> *on Saturday, November sixth*
> *at eight o'clock*
> *The Plaza*
>
> *R.s.v.p.*
> *700 East 69th Street*   *Dancing*

If a regular engraved "invitation card" is used, the parents' name, the function, daughter's name and other pertinent matter, as well as the guest's name, is handwritten. Obviously a third-person invitation requires a formal reply, such as:

> *Mr. and Mrs. Henry Blank*
> *accept with pleasure*
> *the kind invitation of*
> *Mr. and Mrs. John Henry Doe*
> *for dinner*
> *Saturday, November sixth*

Unless they live or move in a strictly temperate community, it is usual for the debutante's parents to serve champagne and sometimes other liquor at her party. Since, even though many older guests are present, this is a party for young people, the wise host and hostess are careful to limit the amount of liquor available to the "junior group." In a choice between being considered "stingy" and permitting young men and women too easy access to liquor, I'd choose the former any time. A plentiful supply of soft drinks, tomato juice and so on should also be easily available.

Subscription dances are always well chaperoned. They have the ladies of the various committees, a floor committee (usually made up of mature men) and a group of ushers. The latter are to see that no young men get out of hand, to dance with girls who seem stranded and so on. Since they are young and want to enjoy the dance, the members of the floor committee take up where they leave off. The parents who give a private party for their daughter should remember that it is her party and that they must be present throughout. They must have a sense of responsibility toward their daughter and her friends. They can't turn over the party to the young people. They and a few of their close friends should unobtrusively fill the roles of chaperon and floor committee. Thus they will do their part to counteract the bad publicity that has been spread about such parties.

Those invited to a debutante party, like all guests, have a responsibility toward their hostess. They should acknowledge the invitation promptly. They should arrive as indicated and dressed appropriately. At a big ball, men wear white tie and tails and girls wear formal evening dresses. At a small dance, dinner jackets and less elaborate evening dresses are correct. It is usual for older friends and young men to send flowers to the debutante. Sometimes close women friends and older relatives give her personal gifts. Whether it is a ball or a party at home, guests must remember their manners, must conduct themselves like ladies and gentlemen.

There are two other rather old-fashioned ways of presenting a daughter. One is a luncheon for girls and older women; the other is for the girl's mother or older woman relative to send out her visiting card with the debutante's name below her own. The latter is not unusual if there has been a recent death in the family or in the case of a girl whose parents are dead. However, a girl must have a big family circle or come from a family well known in the community in order to be invited to other debutantes' parties if either a luncheon or visiting card is her sole "presentation."

Whether she is presented at a big ball or a small private dance, the debutante's dress is white and cut on conservative lines. She should remember that she is "on display" and her manners should be correct, her grooming perfect.

It is useless to say that debutantes and debuts are now passe. Useless, too, to point out that, since the average girl has had dates and been to dances before her eighteenth birthday, there is no meaning to the debut.

The fact remains that the girl whose schoolmates are introduced to society will want to go right along with the custom. In addition, debutante parties mean business for shops, caterers, florists, hotel banquet managers, orchestras. I won't say that a debut is important unless it is important to the girl who wants it. But I will point out that, just as not all our young people go to high school or college proms, so not all young women are interested in making a debut. If it is what her friends do, if she enjoys formal dances, if her parents can afford it and the charity that benefits is worthwhile, I see no reason for criticizing the debutante. Her particular coming out party may not introduce her to the inner circle of her community's social life, but if it introduces her to her circle, if she makes a few friends, stores up a few pleasant memories for the future, the party is worth the expense.

21

The Engaged Couple

THE MODERN GIRL usually knows in advance that a marriage proposal is in the offing. No longer does a man propose on bended knee and, accepted, take a solitaire from his pocket and slip it on the young lady's finger. Frankly, I've never taken that version of the "honorable proposal" very seriously. I'm sure that even in the days when a young woman was always chaperoned, when she was seldom alone with a man for more than a few stolen minutes, she always *sensed* when a friendship was a romance and when it was friendship— and nothing more.

Whether they have gone through school together or their meeting is fairly recent, there is a period in which the young people know that they want to get married. Sometimes they decide that he'll give her the engagement ring on her birthday or at Christmas or when he finishes college. They use today's expression and say they are "going steady." Actually, they are *engaged* from the first time he seriously mentions marriage (even though in the rather distant future) and she consents. They may decide to say nothing about it until he can afford a ring or until he graduates, but the girl who agrees to "become engaged in April" is engaged right then and is no longer free to accept other dates. The ring does not *make* the engagement official. The ring is a symbol of their troth; the engagement is official, even though secret, from the time the girl says "yes."

A diamond solitaire is the traditional engagement ring but it is not the only stone that may be used. The sapphire, emerald, ruby, pearl are popular—in that order. Sometimes the stone is combined with a diamond or diamonds, but when an emerald cut stone is chosen it is often unaccompanied. In lieu of a diamond or other precious stone, a girl may wear her fiancé's class or family crest ring as an engagement ring. And bear in mind that many a happy couple started out without an engagement ring of any kind. (There is a disadvantage in this, however. Some young women insist that they don't want an engagement ring or don't want a "white wedding." After several years of marriage, they speak regretfully about the ring, the white bridal gown and so on that they missed. The girl was the one who urged that they eliminate the luxuries but ten years later the man is made to feel on the defensive because he deprived her of them.)

Far from producing the ring when the girl accepts his proposal, the average modern couple talks over the subject, possibly discussing their preferences in engagement and wedding rings even before he comes right out with a proposal. So, too, it is not unusual for the man to take her along when he goes to buy the ring. (The tactful way to handle this, however, is for him to look at rings, select two or three styles in his price range, have them put aside for her perusal. In this way he avoids the possibility of her "falling in love" with a ring beyond his budget.)

If a solitaire is out of the question, I prefer a college ring, family crest or old ring that has sentimental value. However, some young women want their birthstone—in either a standard or antique setting. (In college I knew a girl whose preference was a gold bangle with their initials and the date made into an engraved design!) Since there is really no rule about engagement rings, you may be as original as you wish —always provided your choice is not gaudy or ostentatious. Here are the stones for each month of the year:

January	Garnet
February	Amethyst
March	Bloodstone
April	Diamond
May	Emerald
June	Agate
July	Ruby
August	Sardonyx
September	Sapphire
October	Opal
November	Topaz
December	Turquoise

Although the girl's family may be expecting an engagement, it is tactful for the young man to speak of their plans to her father. If she is a career girl living away from home, she writes her good news to her parents and encloses a short note from her fiance. Once the girl has consented and her parents have been told, the man tells his parents. Tradition decrees that his mother or nearest woman relative should get in touch with the prospective bride at once. She may telephone or, if at a distance, write and welcome the young woman into the family. The girl should then consult with her mother about having the families meet—if they are not acquainted. If they already know each other, no ceremonial visit is necessary, but regardless of how well she knows the girl, how often she sees her, his mother should make a point of getting in touch with the girl to let her know she is pleased about the engagement. It is to be hoped that this is entirely true. If, as is too often the case, the man's mother is *not* pleased, she should carefully avoid saying so to anyone— even her nearest relatives and closest friends. The girl, for her part, may realize that his mother is not overenthusiastic about the engagement, but she should strive to maintain some degree of friendly relationship. It is foolish to say "I'm marrying Bill, not his family." Although this is true, it is also true that there are enough problems in marriage without starting off with a handicap caused by veiled unpleasantness between the bride and her mother-in-law.

After the immediate families have been told the happy news, the girl's parents make the announcement. An engagement may be announced at a tea, dinner, cocktail party or informal evening get-together. The invitations to such a party must *not* mention the engagement, however, for if the purpose is to announce it when all guests have arrived, it is rather pointless to mention it in advance.

In society circles and in small towns it is customary to send the announcement of the engagement to the society editor of the newspaper or, in a city, newspapers. This is usually sent out with a note that it is for publication on the day after the party. For help in wording an engagement announcement, read the announcements in any large city newspaper. There is little variation in the wording and any of them can be fitted for the individual case.

Those who do not mingle in society groups or who do not want the announcement to appear in the papers should telephone or write the news to relatives and close friends.

Actually, whether a society item is printed or the engaged couple and their families write letters and phone, the most popular way of spreading the news is by word of mouth.

Printed or engraved engagement cards and paid announcements in the newspaper are not good form.

Since no mention of the engagement is made in the invitation to the party, guests say nothing about it even though they suspect that an announcement will be made. The girl's father, mother or nearest relative makes the announcement after all guests have arrived. The guests congratulate the young man, his parents and his fiancee's parents. Traditionally, the bride is wished happiness, not congratulated—since this would imply "she got her man," and courtesy decrees that we assume that he won her!

The man's mother or a close relative of the girl may give her a personal gift, but other gifts are not in order. This is not a general gift occasion.

Whether they are engaged, "going steady" or married, let's face it, it is the woman who sets the standard of their social conduct. With this in mind, the engaged girl avoids constant hand-holding, pet names, constant displays of affection in the presence of others. Their friends are willing to believe they are in love without obvious reminders, and no man's mother *ever* enjoyed watching him act moonstruck over a girl. Naturally, the engaged girl won't go on an unchaperoned overnight trip with her fiance. She won't travel alone with him to a resort hotel, even though she may plan to spend at least part of her vacation in the area where he is spending his. Above all, she won't spend too much unchaperoned time in his apartment if he lives alone. A girl, engaged or not, is her own best chaperon, and if she is old enough to be engaged she is sufficiently adult to know that unchaperoned visits in his flat can cause gossip.

It might be well to note here that in our modern day it is considered permissible for two girls to go to dinner with two men in a bachelor's apartment, for two girls to go to a resort together and spend a great deal of time with two men friends who, preferably, are not in the very same hotel, or at least have rooms far removed from the girl's room. But it is *not* considered good form for one girl and man to travel together or stay at the same hotel. (Each couple "chaperons" the other.)

If the man is working in another city, away at college or spends a great deal of his time studying, his fiance must be doubly careful to avoid criticism or gossip. Even if she has not received her ring, she should not accept invitations from other men. Obviously this rule (in reverse) applies to her fiance also.

If parents approve of the match, have sufficient money and want their offspring to continue in college or graduate school, I'd favor marriage on a tight budget for students, rather than a long engagement. If lack of money makes this impossible, a two-year or three-year engagement is the alternative. Frankly, I don't think the engagement should be formally announced until within a year of a possible wedding. On the other hand, I think family and intimate friends could be told and the man may give his fiancee his class ring or fraternity pin if he cannot afford an engagement ring. I don't think a long engagement works out with a more mature couple. If a man and woman are both working and see each other frequently they can drift into a routine of going to expensive restaurants, shows and so on. The man who puts off marriage because he wants to buy a new car, who postpones it again because he wants to go on a cruise is looking for excuses to avoid settling down. The long engagements I refer to are difficult enough and are only feasible for young people who are studying and working toward a goal.

There is no reason to be shocked at the news of a broken engagement, yet too many of us act as if it were a tragedy. The engagement period is a time of adjustment, a time to study and evaluate each other. It is too bad if it must be terminated, but it is better to find out *before* marriage than after.

No matter who terminates the engagement, the girl returns the ring and any gifts of real value. In addition, she returns to his family any jewelry or articles of sentimental value that they may have given her. If she has received many gifts at showers, she asks the individual givers if they will accept them back. Although some women feel they want their shower gifts returned, others take the attitude that they bought them for the girl and "if she can't use them now, she may be engaged again" and resent the suggestion that they take them back. After all, she has terminated her engagement, not her friendship, so those who gave her shower gifts are the ones to decide what is to be done with them.

The girl who has broken her engagement, her parents and her family should carefully avoid criticizing the young man, discussing the breakup, blaming his mother or in other words "airing their private business." Anyway, it sounds ridiculous to speak of his mean temper, his uncouth habits, his lack of manners. If she took a year or two to discover that he was so impossible, it doesn't say much for her. Even more than the girl, the man must be careful to avoid mention of her name. If he talks about her it marks him not a gentleman, and acquaintances will think she is well rid of him.

It goes without saying that no well-bred person asks questions about a broken engagement. It is never polite to pry into the affairs of others, and only a gossip would take advantage of another person's pent-up feelings to ask intrusive questions about anything so personal. We are told the engagement has been canceled and do not refer to it again. If, as is sometimes the case, a society editor prints an item about it, the wording is usually "by mutual consent." One who sees this in the paper or hears of it from a neighbor should not phone or write to the girl or her mother either to express sympathy or to try to find out details.

22

The Trousseau and Hope Chest

THE MODERN YOUNG man and woman go into marriage with their eyes open. Despite their youth, most of the young people realize that they can't expect to start off in the style to which parents' incomes have made them accustomed. They realize, too, that although money isn't everything, it is rather important, especially if you lack it. Therefore, they discuss the subject of finances, budgets and basic needs before they are married. And since for most of them every dollar is important, they are glad to receive "practical" wedding presents.

As soon as she is engaged, the modern girl starts thinking about a trousseau. This, in itself, is far different from earlier days. Before the First World War, the average girl's trousseau was to great extent collected by her mother. A girl who was born to wealth received table and flat silver to mark her birthdays. By the time she was twenty-one, she might have a complete silver service. It was, of course, in this era that silver was marked with the bride's *maiden* initials. After all, how else could you initial the coffee spoons you gave to a thirteen-year-old? Silver, possibly heirloom china, monogrammed linens were put aside as the start of the young girl's trousseau. (The word "trousseau" comes from the French *trousse,* and means a "little bundle." Thus "trousseau" meant the little bundle of worldly goods with which a bride started her married life.)

Just as families of wealth started collecting silver, those of average income collected linens, possibly handmade afghans, other household necessities. These were stored in a mothproof chest, which was referred to as a "hope chest."

When young women started pursuing careers instead of only pursuing possible husbands, they tired of collecting household linens for a home they might never possess. In addition, the stored linens often turned yellow, or at least seemed "old" and old-fashioned when the time arrived to use them.

The modern young woman, if she buys a chest at all, only does so when she is engaged. Sometimes a fiance purchases this as a gift, but this is more a European than an American custom. So, too, she only starts collecting her trousseau when she knows whom she is going to marry and what her early married life will be like. If the bride and bridegroom are going to Africa as missionaries for two years, there is little point in buying blankets, bone china or embroidered lawn place mats. If they will live and study at a college and rent a small furnished apartment, bed linens, towels and stainless steel cutlery, a radio and typewriter, are indicated. If they will embark on their married life in a smart city apartment or a ranch house of their own in the "right" suburb, they'll have to plan on entertaining and will therefore need more of almost everything.

The following suggestions are entirely flexible; each bride must decide what and how much she needs. However, I may point out that far too many engaged girls completely forget such mundane items as pot holders, dust cloths and glass towels when they shop for their future home.

Kitchen Needs: Two to six towels (depending on whether there will be a dishwasher and on whether the bride believes in "drying" or "draining dry" the dishes), about three glass towels, two pot holders, six dust cloths, several cleaning cloths, a silver-polishing cloth. Other items are two or three hand towels (a paper towel and rack can substitute), ironing board cover (be sure to get an ironing board, even if only a folding travel one) and a whisk broom.

Bathroom Needs: Six face towels (linen or huck), six to twelve terry hand towels, six bath towels, six to ten wash cloths, two bath rugs and mats, one set shower curtain and bathroom window curtains, six guest towels. (The latter will undoubtedly be received as gifts, so postpone buying any until the last possible minute.)

Dining and Entertaining Needs: Obviously the bride who starts out with a dining room will need more linens than one who eats breakfast and other "family meals" at a little table in a kitchenette or at a counter in a modern compact kitchen and only sets a formal table or buffet in the living room or foyer on rare "company" occasions. If she has an extension or refractory table, she'll need one large damask cloth, possibly a lace banquet cloth, one colored linen or novelty cloth, at least two sets of place mats (these are six to eight to a set), one or two tray cloths, one dozen dinner napkins, one dozen smaller napkins (for use with place mats), one dozen cocktail or tea napkins.

Bedroom Needs: For each bed, allow three pairs of sheets, one heavy or electric blanket and one light-weight blanket, three pairs of pillow cases (for single beds, four pillow cases each will suffice), one mattress cover, one comforter or quilt.

In making any purchases for the future home, and this applies especially to the linen supply, quality is more important than quantity.

The bride's personal trousseau is usually purchased in the few weeks before the wedding. Naturally, what she buys depends upon her social life, what basic clothes are already in her wardrobe, and her future plans. Styles change so rapidly that it is not advisable to buy too many dresses and hats in advance.

Outer Garments: A good fur or winter coat is a boon regardless of the season in which she is married. This eliminates one expense in the first year of the marriage. In addition, she'll need, depending on the season of the wedding, one spring or all-weather coat, one suit or three-piece costume, two afternoon dresses, two or three casual or all-purpose dresses, one dinner dress, one evening dress (optional, of course), two hats, one afternoon (dress) hat, one evening coat or wrap (optional), sweaters, blouses, skirts. Two pairs daytime shoes, one pair (at least) dress shoes, one pair evening slippers. (Sports clothes, raincoat and so on may be added if required.)

Lingerie and Accessories: Three slips or two slips, one half-slip, evening slip (if needed), four bras, one evening bra, four to six nightgowns or pairs of pajamas, four to six pairs of daytime hose, two pairs of evening or very sheer hose, four pairs of day wear gloves, two pairs of "dress" gloves (for formal afternoon and evening wear), one pair long evening gloves, one to two dozen handkerchiefs, two or three pocketbooks for day use, one dress bag for afternoon use, one evening bag. (If black is chosen, it may be possible for one bag to serve for formal afternoon use as well.) One pair bedroom slippers, one robe, housecoat or hostess gown, intimate apparel according to individual preferences.

It is well to remember that the bridegroom, too, should "stock up" on wearing apparel before the wedding.

Linens and silver are marked with either a single initial (the last name) or the complete initials. In former years, it was customary to use the maiden initial (or initials) of the bride. (As I have pointed out, this stemmed from the fact that a girl often had a complete set of silver for twelve before she had a husband to help her use it!) Nowadays, while both forms are correct, the trend is toward marking household goods with the bride's future initials. Thus Mary Jane Doe expects to marry John Henry Brown and her future initials will be "M.D.B."

When a bride is faced with a name such as "O'Connell," "Van Lean," "McCurd" or "de Kourtz" her problem is, should I use "O'C" or just "O?" Most reliable authorities suggest that this is a matter of space. If there is room for it "O'C" is preferred. However, when the "Van" is capitalized, the "V" alone is sufficient. When the name is "de K" or "du L" and space permits, "deK" or "duL" should be used. However, when the letters are to be used in a monogram, only the very first letter (under which the name is listed in directories) is used. (The only exception being names starting with a small letter as "deLacey." In this case, I advise trying to work "deL" into the monogram.)

23

Bridal and
Other Showers

ALTHOUGH IN CONSERVATIVE society showers have always
been considered in dubious taste, most girls enjoy giving
and attending them (up to a point) and look forward to
being showered when they become engaged. In addition,
many of the very young brides of today are marrying young
men still in college or graduate school, certainly not far up
on the success ladder, so the "loot" the girl receives from
her classmates, co-workers or family friends may be of extreme importance to her. Then there are the girls who, although they know the prospective bride doesn't need their
shower gifts, also know that she'll enjoy a lunch or cocktail party in her honor and the gifts given under these circumstances are really "for kicks." At any rate, with all these
things considered, it looks as if the shower is here to stay.

A member of the girl's or her fiance's immediate family
may not openly sponsor a shower for her. This sometimes
poses a problem if no friend volunteers to do so. The solu-

tion, although devious, is still socially ethical. The engaged girl's mother or sister may tactfully suggest to a friend of the girl that they'll absorb the expenses, do the work, supply the refreshments and so on if the friend is willing to let the invitations go out in her name. Sometimes the friend suggests that the party be given in her home. More often, she had not mentioned a shower because she is not situated so that she can give one, but she can "sponsor" a surprise shower in the prospective bride's home or at the home of an agreeable relative. The invitations, of course, go out in the friend's name and she is to all intents and purposes the hostess.

If possible, invitations should be sent out about two weeks before the date and should state exactly what type of shower is planned. They may not, however, specify what each prospective guest must bring! (It is never permissible to give a "silver" or "money" shower for an engaged girl.) Although the invitations may be telephoned, a part of the fun of showers is involved in the trimmings, the gimmicks, the decorations, so if possible gay "shower" invitations should be mailed.

Men should not be invited to a bridal shower, although if the party is held in the evening, the women may be invited for eight o'clock and the shower gifts opened and admired. They are then put away and when the men, who have been invited to come at nine-thirty, arrive, the refreshments are served and it is turned into a general party.

Since all who are invited to a bridal shower are expected to buy a gift, only friends of the engaged girl should be asked. It is not fair to ask young women who hardly know her, friends of the one who gives the shower, and so on. So, too, it is unfair to ask any girl to more than two showers for the same prospective bride.

Shower gifts should not be too expensive. A tray is fine—a complete electric mixer is more appropriate as a wedding present. A silver-handled knife to cut the wedding cake is a novel and pleasant gift. A silver sugar and cream set is too ostentatious—another wedding present. When we consider that most of the girls who attend the shower will also be invited to the wedding and therefore have to send a wedding gift, it is obvious why we discourage too expensive shower presents.

The shower given by co-workers at business or at a nearby restaurant differs from "social" showers in that it is not necessary to invite the girl's or her fiance's mother; often men co-workers are included; and the usual custom is to "take up a collection" and buy one substantial gift.

A stork shower is another "all-women" party. Contrary to a rather widespread impression, the stork shower should *not* be given before the baby's birth. It is a simple afternoon gathering, usually for relatives and very intimate friends only, and often the new baby is brought in for the guests' admiration. Gifts should be articles to supplement the infant's wardrobe. (In buying for a new baby, it is not necessary to buy everything in the smallest size. Babies grow, you know, and the average young mother finds the baby has outgrown some of the gifts before he has worn them!)

In some communities, if the minister's salary is small, it is customary to give a shower for the new minister in order to refurbish the parsonage or rectory. Frankly, I've always found this a trying kind of gathering, but it is one party that the men should be urged to help with and attend. I might add that, when possible, this might be a "silver shower," but it certainly should not be a way of unloading the worn furniture, the old-fashioned accessories that the parishioners don't want. If gifts rather than money are given, they should be *new* and attractively wrapped.

Sometimes an elderly couple moving from a full-sized house to a small apartment are "showered" by their children, relatives and friends. In this case, they may be given the same type of presents that are given to a young couple just starting out. "Silver" or "dollar" showers are also permissible in this case or if the couple, remaining in their home, need repairs or painting done, a money shower is permissible. Bear in mind, however, that only relatives should be invited to this kind of shower and that it should be a party and as festive as possible.

24

The Wedding

WHETHER THE CEREMONY takes place in a cathedral, a tiny chapel in a poor neighborhood, a hall, hotel, the municipal building or town hall, at home or in a garden setting, all weddings have one thing in common—dignity. The wedding that lacks dignity is worse than a display of poor taste—it is offensive to most of us.

The kind of wedding must depend on the finances of the bride's family or, if she is "on her own," *her* finances. A church is the favored locale, although those of the Jewish faith often prefer a hotel setting, with a rabbi officiating. The church ceremony is usually followed by a reception elsewhere. This is also true if the Jewish ceremony takes place in a temple.

Much misunderstanding, worry and needless expense can be saved if the engaged girl and her fiance talk over their views about a wedding, then discuss the matter with their parents or closest relatives. Too often, however, the man says "Anything you want" or "You settle the details," and then, prodded by his mother, makes suggestions *after* wedding plans have been fairly well settled. After the bride's father has paid a deposit on the ballroom in a given hotel is *not* the time to suggest a small wedding and reception limited to the families! One other point that must be settled before any real plans can be made concerns the faith of the clergyman who will officiate. It is usually only a minor detail if both are of the same religion (as if both, though Protestants, are of different sects). If one is either Jewish or Roman Catholic, however, the question of the faith in which they will be married can be of vital importance.

Having amicably settled on the church or religion in which they'll exchange vows, the couple should decide how large and how formal a wedding and, practical touch, how much it should cost. (It is true that in the United States the bride or her family assumes the costs of the wedding and reception, but the bridegroom should be consulted. It is just possible that he would prefer his bride to keep some money in her own bank account, rather than "shoot the works" on a big formal wedding.)

The truly formal wedding, with canopy on church door, carpet "runner" to the curb, organist, soloist and extensive floral decorations throughout the church, is usually followed by a seated wedding breakfast or, in some sections, dinner. To the cost of the meal must be added the orchestra fee, appropriate gifts for the members of the bridal party, and various incidentals. The young people on a budget, the boy and girl still in college, should give some serious thought to just how formal, large and lavish a wedding and reception they want.

In addition to the strictly formal wedding and reception, there are fortunately some variations on the "white wedding" that can still be managed by the couple on a budget. One is the quiet ceremony with only family and very close friends present. This is followed by a home or hotel suite wedding reception, with a typical light buffet or afternoon tea menu, a traditional wedding cake and a champagne toast to the couple. (This type of wedding is often favored by those of different faiths, since the attendance at the ceremony is limited and attention is focused on the informal reception.)

Frankly, I'm not enthusiastic about the second type, which consists of a semi-formal church wedding, with bride in white, several attendants and the men in formal clothes. This is followed by a reception or lunch for the bridal party and immediate families only. My feeling is that the bride who eliminates the reception should also cut down on the "trimmings" of the ceremony.

Still another form of church wedding is that in which the bride wears white but not a traditional wedding dress; the bridegroom and best man wear dark business suits; and there is one attendant. This ceremony is restricted to the families and close friends and there is no reception. In fact, after such a wedding it is not unusual for the couple to say good-by to their families at the church door and leave at once on their honeymoon.

The prospective bride must bear in mind that her bridal gown is the keystone of the wedding. What kind of gown, material, style and degree of formality she chooses must govern the dresses of the attendants and the attire of the men in the bridal party. If she selects white satin with a cathedral train, she must have at least two bridesmaids in addition to her honor attendant. For a wedding before six in the evening, the men must wear morning coats and gray striped trousers. After six, it is considered an evening wedding and formal clothes (white tie and tails) are in order. For them to wear dinner jackets (tuxedos) at a morning wedding or business suits and white ties (it's been done!) at an evening wedding would be incongruous and no more dignified than a three-ring circus.

Naturally, the man and woman far from home or with no family ties may decide to be married in the City Hall, in a judge's chambers, or in the parlor of a country justice of the peace. The bride and her one attendant wear simple dresses or suits; the bridegroom and best man wear business suits. It is far from romantic, but it is just as legal and binding as a ceremony performed by a bishop. Since this is really a simple "marriage" the etiquette rules pertaining to "weddings" don't really apply.

The hour of the ceremony decides the type of wedding reception or, more correctly, the wedding "repast." Roman Catholics are encouraged to have a formal wedding at noon, although ten and eleven o'clock are equally popular morning hours. Such a ceremony is followed by a "wedding breakfast," which is actually a lunch.

The evening or very late afternoon are favorite times for Jewish weddings. In either case, a dinner menu is usual.

Four o'clock is the fashionable hour for most Protestant weddings that take place in the afternoon. A light repast, similar to a tea menu, is in order.

Most of us think of a church when we speak about a wedding, but this is not the only setting. Although it is possible to have the marriage performed at home, few of us today have homes that are sufficiently large. Certainly, each year there are fewer garden weddings because there are fewer gardens that lend themselves to a fairly large wedding and reception. (And if the wedding is to be limited to families only, why not economize all the way and have the ceremony performed in the living room?) Actually, for a simple wedding, sans bridesmaids and ushers, a large living room will do—if you are lucky enough to have or borrow the use of one. A room or suite of rooms in a hotel is, as I have mentioned, a popular choice. Such a room is usually referred to as a "public room" or "banquet room." It is not as large as the ballroom but can accommodate the average wedding or wedding reception. Of course, if you are a member or can obtain guest privileges from a member, a private club is the ideal place for the reception and also works out very well as a place for the ceremony, once you've ruled out a church setting.

As soon as you decide where you would like to have the ceremony performed, go into action about it. The girl who dreams of being married in a certain church may, much to her consternation, find out that it has already been reserved for another wedding at that time. The same is true about a wedding in a temple or hotel—or even an informal wedding in a judge's chambers. If you select a big hotel, it may be possible to get substitute reservations if the room you want is already booked. A small hotel or club may have only one room for this purpose and if it is already reserved for your date you'll have to change the date or the locale of the wedding. Remember, it is never "too early" to get in touch with the one you want to perform the ceremony or to try to reserve the place of your choice.

It is usual to have the church wedding performed in the bride's parish church. She also selects the clergyman unless the bridegroom has a relative or close friend and he wants to have him either perform the ceremony or assist at it.

Just as the engagement announcement is sent out by the bride's family, relative or very close friend, so the wedding and reception is traditionally "sponsored" by "her people."

The only exception to this rule is when a bridegroom's clergyman father is a pastor and the young man wants to be married by him and in his church. Even in the case of a girl with no relatives, the wedding reception may be in the home of a relative or friend of the bridegroom, but not in the home of the bridegroom's parents. If the girl lacks money, too (let's hope her beauty and charm are in abundance!), the man's family may "pick up the tab" for the reception, but they must not obviously "run everything" or pay for everything.

Decorations for the church and place of the reception may be as costly as you wish or held down to a minimum if necessary. However, it is well to bear in mind that a formal church wedding in a city calls for floral decorations for altar, possibly the chancel, side altars and so on. In addition, it is not unusual to have white flowers at the end of each pew. The sensible course here—and in fact in any city church wedding—is to tell the florist approximately what you would like and what you want to spend for the decorations. Very often the florist who decorates the church can also take care of the flowers for the reception. Sometimes, however, the hotel insists that their florist take care of the latter.

In the country you can sometimes decorate the church with flowers from your own and friends' gardens. If the reception is at home, you can do your own decorating, but even in the country or suburbs the local hotel or club manager may prefer that a specified florist do all the work on the premises.

White flowers are, of course, traditional for the first marriage. Although the woman who is being married for the second (or seventh?) time sometimes prefers colored blossoms, in my opinion white should always be used on the altar. The stark white effect might be broken by green leaves, but since it is usual to have less decorations for a "repeat" marriage (for instance, bunches of flowers on each pew; white ribbon to close the pews just before the processional is only for the first wedding) a few vases of white blossoms and green leaves lend a touch of bridal splendor and dignity to the scene. This is especially true if the bride wears a simple colored afternoon dress. White is for the "first time" bride, to be sure, but we are dressing up the altar, not the bride.

The late afternoon (about five o'clock) or evening wedding may be candlelit, but although flickering wax candles may be beautiful and very romantic looking, there is a definite danger involved. For this reason, clergymen usually discourage this touch. On the other hand, it is often possible for a large florist company or a caterer to supply silver candlesticks with "wax candles" that have tiny bulbs, are run on batteries, and give an illusion of being the real thing. The bride who has her heart set on being lighted down the aisle by a procession of candle-bearing attendants might give a little thought to this version of the candlelit ceremony.

One of the things to discuss with the officiating clergyman is the subject of music. Most large churches have regular organists and usually prefer that you engage the services of the organist if, as is usual at most weddings, you want organ music. Obviously, the music must be dignified and appropriate. In most Roman Catholic and many Episcopal churches they have rules regarding what hymns may be played. If the organist is not connected with the church or has any doubts about your selections, talk over this matter with the clergyman well before the wedding. For a home or hotel wedding you may have a rented organ, a string ensemble or recorded hymns, or, at a simple home ceremony, an obliging friend may play the piano. (I'm rather dubious about this, although it has been done successfully. Too often the amateur gets stage fright, and a wrong note can echo and re-echo through the hushed room. Too, I find it hard to combine a friendship with a business arrangement. If the pianist is late, you can't say anything. She is doing you a favor. If she decides to play her own selection, rather than yours, what can you do! Bear in mind, also, that other guests who would not go near a professional musician will feel free to gather at the piano since her presence gives an informal "homey" touch to the atmosphere.)

For a church wedding or the wedding held in a large hall or hotel room, the rule is that the left side (as you face the altar) is for the bride's family and the right is for the family of the bridegroom. At a home or hotel wedding, guests may not adhere strictly to this rule, but they do remember to leave a "middle aisle" and leave space "up front" for the families.

Whether it is a big, formal church wedding or a simple home one, the bride's mother is the last to take her place. Her entrance is the signal that the wedding is about to begin and those who arrive after her slip into the first vacant place they see in the rear.

In this country, as in many others, white has always been reserved for the "first time" bride. Her flowers, too, are white, although occasionally a bride likes one tiny blue or pink flower in the center of the bouquet or carries a combination of white blossoms and ivy.

Although white satin is correct for any season, there are other materials from which to choose—shantung, crepe, chiffon, linen, taffeta, silk organza, organdy, velvet, brocade —to name a few. Let us not overlook the synthetics, which are sometimes used with outstandingly beautiful results.

The bridal veil is always the color or shade of the dress. It is important that you "put the two together" if you're contemplating wearing a new dress and an heirloom veil. "White is white"—but only to a degree. Among the "shades" of white are "off-white," "oyster white," "cream," "champagne," "pure white." In addition there are some with a bit more definite color—"wheat," "ice white" (which is sometimes called "blue-white") and "blush" (which is white with an illusion of pink tone). The bride who can afford it sometimes chooses a mantilla of fine lace or, if she is lucky, she may wear a veil that has been worn by brides in her or the bridegroom's family. If wearing that special veil means something, take it along when shopping for the wedding dress. In this way you can be sure they will match.

If possible, the bridal slippers are of the material of the dress. Otherwise satin, peau de soie or silk shantung is the usual choice, although brocade or linen may be used. Most brides choose very light beige or flesh tone hose.

There is a wide variety of white flowers from which to choose and there are several bouquet styles. Since the style and size of the bouquet depend upon the style of dress and height of the bride and since the flowers used will depend upon the amount spent, I really think the wise course is to give the florist a good description of the dress, exact shade and style, and let him make suggestions on bouquets.

Ideally, the bride should not wear gloves. However, this depends on fashion, length of sleeve, and the bride's preference. If she wears gloves, the left should be removed or the "ring finger" ripped or cut so that the ring can be easily slipped on.

Before she leaves home, the bride should remove her engagement ring. It is usually transferred to the right hand, as there can be no ring on the finger on which the wedding band is placed. After the ceremony, she may return the engagement ring to its place—*above* the wedding ring.

It is not feasible to suggest going-away costumes since what she wears will depend upon her honeymoon plans, mode of travel, finances and the time of year. She usually tries to avoid a too conspicuously new look, extreme style or "loud" colors. This is primarily planned to avoid being "spotted" as a newly married couple wherever they go. The notion is good, but it seldom works. Newlyweds are almost always recognized as "just married."

As she stands dressed in her bridal finery, the thought occurs "What of the old wedding superstition—something old, something new, something borrowed and something blue?" It really doesn't mean anything—yet how few brides ignore its admonition? So, with the help of her mother and the intimates who surround her, she checks it off—the "new" is her dress, the "borrowed" is the veil, the "old" is a family pin or the pearls on her neck, and the "blue" is a blue flower or initial on her handkerchief. All will be well, for she conforms to the ridiculous but well-loved superstition of brides.

The bride selects the dresses of her attendants, but each girl pays for her own. With this in mind, the considerate bride considers their finances and chooses accordingly. Obviously, if she is fabulously wealthy and wants her attendants dressed in shepherds' frocks or Grecian gowns that they can't wear again, she should consider the dresses as "costumes" and pay for them. But this advice is intended for the average bride who wants a lovely wedding but still must consider money—her own and that of her attendants. So she picks a style and material that the girls can wear later.

The style of dresses selected for the attendants, the materials and styles, length of skirt and sleeves must depend on the wedding gown, formality of wedding, and time of year. The attendants' dresses should be alike in material and style. If it is fashionable to have them all wear the same color, they should do so. Different colors or shades should only be decided upon if there are at least six attendants. Then, since the attendants will walk in pairs, girls who are paired should have the same color. The honor attendant and flower girl or junior bridesmaid may wear contrasting colors or they may wear the same color as the bridesmaids but with contrasting accessories.

Since color is a part of the fashion picture and fashion changes, it is not possible to suggest definite colors, but bear in mind that warmer, richer colors may be worn in winter and that lively, though light colors, are associated with spring and summer.

I can't understand why some brides like "all-white" weddings! The attendants should be a background for the bride, and if they are all wearing white, where is the contrast? On the other hand, a winter "white wedding" with attendants' accessories in rich warm colors could be very effective.

The attendants' bouquets should "go with" the bridal bouquet. The flowers may be the same or similar but colored. If the bride carries a bible or prayer book with a flower marker, her attendants may have the same (with colored flowers, of course) or they may carry old-fashioned bouquets or nosegays. Here again, my best advice is "Talk to the florist, tell him the colors and styles of dresses and average height of girls."

Attendants usually wear gloves, either white or dyed to match dresses or accessories. Their slippers are the shade of their dresses or may match accessories. When short-skirted dresses are in style, the attendants' hose should all be the same shade.

Hats or head coverings of some kind are always worn at church weddings. Broad-brimmed hats are seen occasionally but are no longer as "standard" for attendants as they were in former years. The band, cluster of flowers or wreath of ivy that had been associated with evening weddings is now the most popular "hat." Attendants sometimes wear shoulder-length tulle veils dyed to match their gowns, but I feel that the veil should be reserved for the bride and that her attendants should wear other forms of headgear.

It shouldn't be necessary to remind the bride and her attendants that make-up should be natural, almost subdued. Also, this is not the time to try a new hairdo—or a new hair color.

Although much less is written or said about them, the bridegroom and best man are interested in dressing correctly and are entitled to their share of the spotlight, too.

Obviously, what the bridegroom and men in the bridal party wear and the number of ushers needed depends upon the type of wedding the bride has planned—formal, informal, day or evening. If she wants a formal day wedding with six bridesmaids, he persuades at least six of his friends to be ushers. (They are not "escorts" for the bridesmaids and may be either single or married.) If it is an informal wedding, he'll know that two ushers will suffice.

The bridegroom and best man dress exactly alike. The bridegroom's boutonniere may be slightly different. It may be a small flower similar to those in the bride's bouquet, it may be lily-of-the-valley or orange blossom; whereas the best man's flower is a tiny gardenia, white carnation or white rose. The ushers usually wear boutonnieres like that worn by the best man.

Just as the bride selects her attendants from among her closest friends and relatives, so the bridegroom picks his best man and ushers in the same way. If the bridegroom has a sister, she is usually asked to be among the attendants. If the bride has a brother, he is asked to serve as an usher— once in a while he is picked as best man.

In the case of married members of the bridal party, their respective spouses are invited to the wedding and reception. They are seated as near the bridal party's table as feasible, of course.

A strictly formal day wedding calls for morning coats and striped trousers for all the men in the bridal party. With the dress shirts, they may wear gray and black or black and white striped four-in-hand ties, although the old-fashioned ascots are equally correct. Sometimes the bridegroom and best man wear the ascots and the ushers wear ties. The bride's father or the man who gives the bride away wears similar attire, as does the bridegroom's father if he serves as best man. For an informal day wedding, the men wear dark business suits, white shirts and matching solid blue or conservatively striped ties. In summer, white suits or light-colored trousers and dark jackets may substitute for the dark business suit. This is particularly true if the wedding takes place in country or suburb.

Six o'clock is the dividing line between day and evening weddings. A very formal evening wedding calls for formal evening clothes (white tie and tails) for all the men in the bridal party. A semi-formal wedding (these are more usual) means dinner jackets (popularly called "tuxedos") and at an informal wedding the usual business suit is customary.

Partly because we're becoming more casual, partly because a formal wedding is so much more expensive because of the "hidden costs" involved, the popular day wedding nowadays is not the strictly formal but the semi-formal one. The bride's dress is no different, she possibly has just as many attendants, but the men in the bridal party wear stroller (sometimes called "director") jackets with their striped trousers. This type of jacket is to the morning coat what a dinner jacket is to formal evening clothes—one degree less formal but just as dignified. The jacket has the advantage of looking well on most men, whether short and stout or very tall.

If the evening wedding takes place in *late* spring or summer, white dinner jackets may substitute for the standard dark ones. Like the dark ones, they are *not* correctly worn before six in the evening. They may be worn as early as June in the suburbs but only in July and August in the city.

Although there is no limit to the number of attendants and ushers they may have, only two are essential—the honor attendant and the best man. In addition to their duties at the ceremony they are usually the official witnesses of the marriage. The best man complies with the request "Get me to the church on time," and also carries the wedding ring, which he produces when needed. He takes care of tickets, passports, luggage, arranges about the car in which they leave for their honeymoon. He sees that there are no "just married" signs or tin cans attached to the vehicle and, if there are train, boat or plane schedules to worry about, it is his job.

The maid or matron of honor is next in importance, although first so far as the bride is concerned. She usually helps the bride to dress, checks the bride's appearance, takes care of last minute touches to veil, hair or make-up while they are waiting to start down the aisle. At the altar, if the bride wears a "face veil" she may lift it. She takes the bride's bouquet so that the bride's hands are free during the ceremony and, if it is a double-ring wedding, she produces his ring at the proper time.

The bridesmaids' only obligations are to look pretty, be on time, keep step as they walk down the aisle and serve as part of the receiving line at the reception. From time to time, junior bridesmaids are "in fashion," and when they are their duties are just like those of grown attendants. The junior bridesmaids may be from ten to fifteen years old.

The flower girl and ring-bearer have the duties that their titles signify. The little girl (between four and seven years old) walks just ahead of the bride. She carries either a basket of flowers or a nosegay. (Flower girls no longer strew flower petals in the path of the bride.) The ring-bearer at a formal wedding should *not* be dressed in a miniature tail coat or dinner jacket! He should wear either a black eton suit (velvet or dull-finish satin) and white satin, wide collared blouse or a white satin suit. In either case, he wears short white socks and black dress slippers. (Need I comment that it is becoming increasingly difficult to persuade small boys to act as "ring-bearers?") The ring-bearer is supposed to carry a white satin pillow on which rests the wedding ring. Since there is so much danger of the child dropping the ring, we've gone through various cycles in this—the ring was pinned or basted to the pillow (it was difficult to get it "free" when needed) or it was held on the pillow with gummed tape (the ring was sticky when pulled off). Next we evolved the notion of using a dummy ring, sewn to the pillow; the real ring was safe in the best man's keeping. Since the little ring-bearer was thus only decorative, his role has been dropped at most weddings. A bride who has a small brother or beloved little nephew may, of course, have him precede her down the aisle with the satin ring pillow.

In England it is not unusual to have all small children attendants. They certainly look attractive and, in many ways, create fewer problems than more mature attendants, but there is always the possibility of a youngster getting stage fright, balking at starting down the aisle or actually crying. With this in mind, I think there is a good deal to be said in favor of older attendants.

The duties of the ushers vary according to the formality of the wedding and the locale. They usually go directly to the church, arriving thirty to forty minutes before the ceremony. They wait just inside the door and, after ascertaining "bride or bridegroom," an usher offers his arm and escorts a lady down the aisle. If there are two ladies, he takes the elder and the younger one follows. In the case of a lady and gentleman, the usher escorts the lady and the gentleman follows, about a step to one side, a half step to the rear of the lady. When a gentleman is alone, the usher walks beside him and indicates the seat he is to take. If the unaccompanied gentleman walks down the aisle alone, he takes a seat well to the rear, since an usher may take a guest forward, but one does not stress one's own importance.

At the reception, ushers do not stand in the receiving line. They make themselves useful, however, by mingling with guests, dancing with the attendants and other ladies present.

At a double wedding, it is usual for all the ushers to walk first, in pairs according to size. They are followed by the bridesmaids, paired according to size. The honor attendant for the first bride follows, then the first bride walking on her father's right. They are followed by the honor attendant for the second bride, who precedes the second bride and her brother, uncle or whoever is to escort her down the aisle.

No matter how small the wedding, and certainly if it is a big formal one, a rehearsal is important. This is usually two or three days before the wedding, although if many of the bridal party come from out of town, it may take place the day before. In smart social circles, the bride's parents or (more often) the bridegroom's parents give a dinner either before or after the rehearsal. All members of the bridal party, with the exception of the bride, rehearse their roles. The bride watches while a substitute "walks through her part" and the clergyman makes any needed suggestions. Like the old saying "something old, something new," the custom of the bride having a substitute rehearse for her is based on superstition. The modern bride who wants to "run through her part" may do so; it may make her less nervous on the Big Day or she may be against superstitions in general.

Bachelor dinners are not nearly as popular as years ago. This stag affair used to be given by the prospective bridegroom. Nowadays, if it is given at all, it is more likely to be a surprise party given for him by the best man or other close friend. The purpose is to "rib" the bridegroom about his loss of liberty, approaching captivity and so on. It is usually given in a restaurant or club. If given in a private home, a woman member of the family may supervise the meal— but from the kitchen, since her presence should not be made known.

At a formal wedding, it is customary for the attendants to assemble at the bride's home and, in cars supplied by the bride's parents, precede her and her father to the church. (Years ago, the attendants dressed in the bride's home!) Nowadays, with our streamlined living, small apartments and general lack of extra room, it is permissible for the attendants to go directly to the church if necessary, although the former is the better arrangement. As I have mentioned, the ushers, properly dressed, go to the church early. The best man calls for the bridegroom, sees that he is properly attired, checks over the details of wedding ring, wallet, tickets and so on and accompanies the bridegroom to the church. (They usually enter by a side door, through the church house or rectory.)

All guests, including the bride's mother and other family members not in the bridal party and the parents and family of the bridegroom, go directly to the church.

The bride's mother usually delays in the rear of the church with the bride until a few minutes before the processional is to start. She is escorted down the aisle by the chief usher or her son if he is one of the ushers. When she is seated in the first pew on the left of the middle aisle, the ushers may enclose the guests' seats with a length of white ribbon, which runs from the first to the last pew set aside for invited guests. Nowadays a white carpet "runner" is seldom put down, but if it is used this is the time to unroll it.

The organ peals out a traditional processional hymn and the bridal march starts. The ushers lead, in pairs according to height. They are followed by the bridesmaids, paired in the same way. The honor attendant is next, unless there are also junior bridesmaids, who precede the honor attendant. If there are both maid and matron of honor, they may walk single file, or dressed exactly alike (slightly differently from the bridesmaids), they may walk together. A flower girl (or flower girl and ring-bearer) follows the honor attendant. Last, the bride, on her father's right arm. Meanwhile, at the first notes of the processional, the bridegroom and best man enter from sacristy or chancel and take their places on the right of the head of the middle aisle or at the chancel rail, with the bridegroom on the left of the best man.

At the altar rail or entrance to the altar, the ushers and attendants separate, according to the instructions they received at the rehearsal. Usually the usher on the left takes his place to the left of the chancel or on the left side of the entrance to the altar. The usher on the right goes to the right, bridesmaids separate in the same way and stand in front of the ushers. The honor attendant who is to take the bride's bouquet, fix her veil and so on takes her place to the left of the bride. If there is a second honor attendant she has been assigned a location also on the left side. Children *may* follow the other attendants, but I believe they should be inconspicuously taken in tow by one child's mother and kept in a front pew, possibly just to the left of the pew reserved for the bride's family, until the recessional. If this does not seem feasible, one attendant should be given the responsibility of keeping them occupied or, at least quiet, throughout the ceremony.

When the bride and her father reach the waiting bridegroom, the father relinquishes her to him and takes his place in the pew with the bride's mother. The bride, on the bridegroom's *left* arm, goes forward the remaining few steps to their places. The best man, a step or two to the rear right of the bridegroom, goes to his place on the bridegroom's right.

After the ceremony, the bride and bridegroom turn and with the bride on his right, they lead the recessional down the aisle. They are followed by the flower girl and ringbearer, then the honor attendant and best man; if there's a second honor attendant, she walks alone. Last, the bridesmaids walking with the ushers. It is not incorrect for the best man to leave by the sacristy, pick up his own and the bridegroom's hat and overcoat, and go to the street to see that the car for the couple is ready. However, no matter how they try, the modern bride and bridegroom are delayed at least a little by well-wishers, and the best man has ample time to walk in the recessional, get the hats and coats, and take care of other small details before the couple can get away to the reception.

If the formal wedding takes place in hotel or home, the processional is the same as the church one. There is, however, *no recessional* at such a wedding. At the completion of the ceremony, the bride and bridegroom turn and face their guests to receive their congratulations and good wishes.

The informal wedding can be just as beautiful, just as dignified as a very formal one. There is, of course, less fanfare, there are fewer attendants, the bride's dress is less elaborate—and the expenses are naturally less.

Obviously the reception that follows an informal or semiformal wedding is not as large as the gala that follows a formal one. But the ceremony itself differs only in regard to apparel and the fact that there is no choir or opera soloist engaged to sing at an informal wedding, although there is the usual organ music.

Bear in mind that no "excuse" is needed and no explanation should be made for having an informal wedding. Sometimes it is because the bride actually likes simplicity, sometimes it is because the bridegroom does not want to wear a morning coat, sometimes it is because of illness in one of the families. And, let's face it, very often it is because a wedding with no more than two ushers, two bridesmaids, a maid of honor, and best man is just as binding as the more elaborate one but poses less strain in planning and less strain on the finances of the bride's father.

Possibly more changes have been made in the etiquette of second marriages than in any other phase of wedding etiquette. Twenty years ago the average woman who contemplated a second marriage took for granted that it would be a small and quiet one, with a reception for family and close friends only. Nowadays, urged on by business interests involved, many who are getting married for the second time, in fact some who are contemplating a sixth or seventh "blending," calmly assume that they are entitled to an elaborate wedding, complete with white dress, several attendants, a big reception with dancing and all the trimmings. Those who want to wear white will argue that it is only in *some* countries that white is for the first marriage. They point out that Orientals wear pink, which to them denotes "joy," red is worn in some countries, and so on. This is true, of course, but when an average American is married in the United States, he is married according to *our* traditions. In some countries, the bride paints the soles of her feet red and wears a bell on each big toe! If this is their custom, it is appropriate for them. "White for the first time bride" is our custom. No matter how young she is, the previously married woman who insists on dressing like a bride makes herself ridiculous. What should she wear? Any color other than white. Whether she is married in the day or evening, she may wear a floor-length dress in any becoming shade and either a small matching hat or a short veil dyed to match the dress. If she prefers to wear a street-length dress, she should wear a corsage. With the floor-length dress, she may carry a conservative bouquet—nothing big, gaudy or too bridal-like. Her flowers may be partly white—white orchids with very definite purple centers, a nosegay of blue and white flowers or of rosebuds shading from white to deep pink.

No matter how young she is, even if her first marriage was an elopement, she should not try to make a second or third marriage look like a first one. One attendant and a best man are sufficient, although if it seems necessary she may have two ushers to seat guests but not take part in the processional. Although it is permissible for the bride to be given away, it seems a little absurd for a middle-aged woman to be "given in marriage" by her son. If she is quite young, however, she may be escorted down the aisle by her father or a man relative. In some circles it is not unusual to have children of the first marriage in the bridal party. In the case of a widow this is acceptable, but I frankly think the little products of a broken home should be present as guests only.

If she has not already done so, a widow or divorcee should remove (even from her right hand) her first engagement and wedding rings. Although some women have the engagement stones put in another setting, I think if there are children of the former marriage, these rings might be kept for them.

The woman who is married for the first time, regardless of age, may wear white. My advice is, if she is obviously over thirty-five, beige, deep champagne or any becoming pastel is a better choice. If she can pass for younger, she may wear cream, off-white, champagne, pale wheat, but she should eschew satin and other very bridal-like materials. The older woman should wear a small hat, the younger-looking one may wear a very short veil dyed to match her dress.

In the Jewish ceremony, the parents actually take part. The men present wear hats or yamilkes (skull caps) and instead of the processional formation described in this chapter, the bridegroom, accompanied by his parents, walks up the aisle and takes his place beneath a canopy set up for the ceremony. The officiating clergyman begins the service and at the appointed time the bride and her parents go up the aisle and the bride takes her place beside the bridegroom. Although the bride is not in evidence before the ceremony, if it is in a hotel the bridegroom usually greets the guests and receives their good wishes. Cocktails and canapes are frequently served at this time and a dinner is served after the ceremony. Just as at a Christian or non-religious reception, they may or may not have dancing. There is a cake and frequently a small basket or paper cup of candies is at each place at the table.

Since the conduct of the guests can have a great deal of bearing on the dignity of the wedding, it often seems that most of the advice should be directed to them. Well-bred guests do not try to get out of the church before the bridal party. The parents and those in the front pews follow immediately after the ushers and bridesmaids, then the occupants of each pew go out in their turn. The car to take the bride and bridegroom to the reception should be waiting, and it is not good form for guests to delay the couple's departure. (If they are not having a big reception, they should try to arrange to greet their friends in the parish hall or a room off the church. A group milling around the bride and bridegroom in the vestibule is very bad form.)

Ideally, the bride has her "wedding dress" pictures taken before the wedding. In the case of a bride who intends to send her picture and announcement of the wedding to the local paper, this is necessary. If for some reason she does not have her picture taken in advance, the couple should have their pictures and bridal group pictures taken at the reception (possibly in a separate room). It is not good form for the guests to have to wait at the place of the reception while the bridal party goes to a photographic studio.

Weddings are expensive. In this country, the bride's parents traditionally defray most of the costs involved. In the case of a young woman living away from home or without parents, she assumes the cost of her wedding. Of course, if the bridegroom's parents have a great deal of money and want a big wedding and the bride's parents can't afford it, the young man's parents may underwrite the cost. This, however, should be in the form of a gift to the bride. They should not issue the invitations or in any way imply that they are footing the bill. The bride or her family pay for her dress, her trousseau, household linens, china, silver and glassware, all kitchen equipment and accessories. In addition, they pay all costs of the wedding—flowers, organist, decorations, reception, orchestra (if there is dancing), food and liquors. They pay for the cars to take the bride and her father—also the attendants, bride's mother and often bridegroom's parents—to the church. They pay for the wedding invitations or announcements, bridal photographs, candid camera pictures taken at wedding and the gifts the bride gives to her attendants. They take care of the donation or fee for opening the church, but the bridegroom gives a monetary gift or stipend to the clergyman. The bride's family pays for the bouquets for the attendants and, in society circles, sometimes pays for the bridal bouquet. It is equally correct for the bridegroom to buy this, however, and I like the sentimental custom of his buying the bride's flowers.

The bridegroom pays for the wedding ring (in a double-ring ceremony the bride pays for his ring, of course), the marriage license, corsages for his and the bride's mother, gifts for the best man and ushers, if necessary, a car in which he and the best man go to the church. He pays all the expenses of the honeymoon, unless her parents give them a luxury trip as a wedding present.

Since there are so few home weddings nowadays, there is seldom a chance to display the wedding gifts. However, the prospective bride should show presents to visitors, and it is not incorrect for friends to ask "Have you received any more gifts since I was last here?" If possible, the bride and her mother have a few close friends and relatives to tea or cocktails about ten days before the wedding and, at that time, the gifts may be shown and admired. It goes without saying that a well-bred bride does not mention the *amount* of a check, but it is perfectly correct to say "Uncle Jack gave us a check."

No matter how casually or informally she has been brought up or intends to live, the wise bride keeps a list of gifts and their donors. It can be embarrassing to thank Aunt Jane for the hostess tray that was actually the gift of Mrs. Jones!

A bride never returns or exchanges a gift given by the bridegroom's parents or her own—to avoid hurt feelings and misunderstandings. She may, however, exchange other gifts. I can never understand why anyone gets offended if her gift is exchanged. (I well remember my own consternation when I received three identical crystal vases—all purchased in the same shop!)

25

The Wedding Reception

THE IMPORTANT PHASE of the wedding is, of course, the ceremony. Actually, however, most of us are more interested in
the reception. Watching the ceremony seems like watching a
performance combined with paying respectful attention to
a church service. But we're *part* of the reception and, once
the ceremony is over, we want to enjoy ourselves.

The type and time of the reception must, of course, depend
on the type of wedding ceremony and the time at which it
is performed. Since the reception must follow fairly promptly
after the ceremony, more and more weddings are performed
on Saturdays so that those who go to business can attend
without difficulty. It is bad form to have a noon ceremony
and have the reception several hours later unless the ceremony is limited to the immediate families.

The morning or noon wedding is followed by a "wedding
breakfast" (actually a lunch), the afternoon ceremony is followed by a "reception" with assorted tea sandwiches, chicken-

filled patty shells, champagne, punch or liquor, and, of course, a wedding cake or bride's cake. A ceremony after five o'clock is usually followed by a seated dinner. An evening ceremony is followed by the same type of reception and refreshments as the afternoon one.

The elaborateness of the reception and number of guests invited depend on the wishes and finances of the bride and her family. Regardless of the kind of reception, there is a receiving line. As guests enter they shake hands with the bride's mother, who, as hostess, heads the line, then the bridegroom's parents, the bride and bridegroom and attendants. Guests congratulate the parents and the bridegroom, wish the bride happiness and tell the attendants they look pretty. The bride's father is not usually on the receiving line. As host, he greets guests and steers them toward the line. The best man often assists him and ushers merely mingle with the guests.

When all guests have passed down the receiving line, the couple, their attendants and the parents take their places at the bridal table. At a small reception, there may be only the one table. In this case, the bride's mother, as hostess, sits at one end with the bridegroom's father at her right and the officiating clergyman at her left. The bride's father is at the other end of the table with the bridegroom's mother at his right and the next ranking lady (possibly a grandmother or the clergyman's wife) at his left. The bridal party members are seated along the side of the table with the bride and bridegroom in the center, the bride on his right. If there are very few guests all may be seated at this table or there may be one additional table for guests.

Nowadays, however, the more usual custom is for the bridal party to have a table and have several smaller tables at which guests are seated. In this case, the two tables nearest the bridal table are for the respective parents and family members.

The husbands and wives of married members of the bridal party are always invited to the reception but are not seated at the bridal table. They are seated near or at the parents' table or as near the bridal table as possible.

The bride and bridegroom cut and share the first slice of the bride's cake. Other slices are then cut and served to the guests. The bride's cake, which is always a pound or light cake with white icing, is eaten at the reception. The wedding cake is a dark fruit cake that may be distributed to be taken home, although it is occasionally served also. If, as is generally the case, the "wedding cake" is a two-tier or larger creation, it is customary to have the first tier the bride's cake, with dark fruit (either in a white-coated tin or with white icing) an upper tier.

One of the hard-to-eliminate bridal superstitions is that the girl who takes home and puts under her pillow a piece of dark fruit wedding cake will dream of her future husband!

How long the wedding reception lasts depends on the number of guests, the type of reception (obviously a buffet service of light foods will not last as long as a seated dinner), and whether there is dancing. But all good things, including wedding parties, come to an end, and the reception really ends when the bride tosses her bouquet. It is usual for her to do this just before she leaves the group to change into her going-away costume. It is equally correct, however, for her to slip away and change, then appear, ready to leave and holding her bridal bouquet. At a signal all single attendants and women guests stand (usually in a circle) waiting. The bride tosses the bouquet and the one who catches it will, according to superstition, be the next bride! (This custom, which is followed religiously by brides and the elimination of which would undoubtedly cause a dearth of wedding attendants, is handed down from the French of the fourteenth century. Originally, the bride tossed her garter to the guests. Flowers were soon substituted for the garter, however.) Occasionally a bride tosses her bouquet to the girls, a garter to the single men. The man who catches it is supposed to put it on the leg of the girl nearest him or, more often, on the girl who caught the bouquet. I mention this, not in approval, but because it is a fad that is increasing in sections of the country and a fad that, in my opinion, is meaningless and should be discouraged.

Guests start leaving the reception as soon as the bride and bridegroom have gone. The average reception ends within a half hour after their departure. Sometimes a few congenial guests want liquor after the waiters have stopped serving it. Under no circumstances is it permissible to ask for more or ask the host to order more served. So, too, those who want to continue the fun should go elsewhere. A few merrymakers who don't want to "call it quits" are embarrassing to the host and the management of the hotel or club.

It should not be necessary to reiterate that small children should not be invited to wedding receptions. The bride who allows herself to be talked into including the offspring of all married guests is adding a great deal of expense and a great many problems and is certainly not doing anything for the small folk involved. Of course, the small brothers and sisters of the bride and bridegroom belong at the reception. Sometimes nephews, nieces or cousins, as part of the family, are included. But the average married couple invited should not assume that the invitation includes all their youngsters.

26

*Wedding Invitations
and Announcements*

MOST OF US insist we are not interested in weddings—at least, the weddings of others. We pretend that we don't expect or want to be invited to a co-worker's or a classmate's marriage. But we're all sentimental and, whether or not we admit it, we want to "dance at the wedding." This is the reason almost every wedding leaves at least some hurt feelings. Even clergymen who officiate at so many ceremonies are often "miffed" if the bride does not send an invitation. One minister laughingly admitted, "Honestly, I don't want to go to the reception of every bride whose marriage I perform. But I suppose I'm human enough to be piqued when I'm not invited!" I'm afraid many of us are like him. We say, "I hope Jane won't invite me to her wedding. I can't afford to buy another wedding gift this year." Later, we hear that Jane was a beautiful bride. We're amazed and hurt and our line changes to "We went all through school together and she often spent the night in our house. It certainly wasn't courteous to ignore me. Well, that's modern friendship for you!"

With this in mind, the wise bride makes an early start on her wedding guest list. Obviously there will be some acquaintances—even some relatives, perhaps—whom she can't invite if she has to keep within a budget. This is a problem that most brides have to face. The error to avoid, however, is that of overlooking someone who very definitely *should* be invited. For this reason, the bride must carefully check all family lists—such as address books, Christmas card lists, telephone lists and so on.

The final guest list is a compilation of the lists of the bride, her mother and the bridegroom's mother. Most brides find the best way to handle this is to tell the bridegroom's mother how many she may invite (half the total number of guests). The old-fashioned custom is for the bridegroom's mother to submit the names and addresses of those whom she wants invited, and for the bride and her family (or the bridal consultant, if the wedding is professionally handled) to address all envelopes—the lists having been put together. This has a definite advantage as it gives the bride the names and addresses of the bridegroom's relatives and friends with whom they will later keep in touch, and avoids possible duplication. There is, of course, a disadvantage, too. It makes much more work for the bride. The modern casual practice (especially if the bride is a student or holds a job) is for the bridegroom's mother to take sufficient envelopes and address them. She may give the addressed envelopes to the bride, who, after enclosing the invitations mails them with her own, or the bridegroom's mother may have the invitations, enclosures and so on and mail them out when she has them addressed. Both methods are correct, but, for the girl who has the time, I think the old-fashioned custom is preferable.

A formal wedding calls for formal invitations. A semi-formal or very small wedding does not really require an engraved invitation. The bride or her mother may write personal notes or telephone the invitations about two weeks before the ceremony. In the case of the semi-formal wedding, however, the bride usually prefers to send out the traditional third-person invitation.

The formal invitations should be ordered well in advance and should be mailed about three weeks before the date. They are always on "double page" stationery and the wording is all on the first page. White or cream paper may be used. Although the larger-size invitation is still correct, the trend at present is toward a smaller size that is the same size as the envelope. Thus the engraving is not folded but slipped in the envelope "book fashion." Obviously, since tissues are only placed between invitations to keep them from smearing when freshly engraved, they are correctly removed before the invitations are placed in the envelopes. By that time there is no danger of good engraving or plateless engraving smearing.

The standard wedding invitation form used in the United States has not changed in many years. The names of the bride's parents take up the first line, "request the honour" is on the second line. ("Honour" is always so spelled in formal use.)

Correctly, two envelopes are used with each invitation. The outer bears the name and address of the prospective guest, the inner bears the name alone. This one has no mucilage on the flap.

The bride who has a large church wedding sometimes limits the invitations to the reception. In this case "reception cards" are enclosed with the church invitations sent to these special guests. I always think this draws a sharp line of distinction between two sets of guests. Although the custom is acceptable, I think a more kindly plan is to only invite to the church those who are also invited to the reception. When this form of invitation is used, two lines are added to the wedding invitation:

and afterwards at
Hotel Royal.

The expression "Reception immediately following at Hotel Royal" is now seldom used.

When a bride is being married for the first time and her parents are living (and not divorced), there are no real problems about the wording of the invitation. Any good stationer or jeweler can show samples and take orders for the invitations, reception cards and "At Home" cards if needed. Problems arise when the girl's parents are divorced or one parent is remarried. What is the proper wording? If her father is dead, her mother remarried:

Mr. and Mrs. John Henry Smith

- - - - -

her daughter
Mary Jane Brown, etc.

If her parents are divorced, even if neither has remarried, both their names may not appear on the wedding invitation. Then it is customary for the bride's mother to issue the invitation and the bride's father to give the bride away. If the bride's parents are dead, the invitations may go out in the name of a close older relative or a brother or sister. If there is a difference in last names, the bride's full name should appear in the invitation.

In the case of a second marriage, it is not usual to send out formal invitations. Formal announcements are sent, however.

A wedding invitation may not be addressed "Miss Jane Green and Guest." If the bride wants to invite Miss Green's date, she should find out his name and send him an invitation. So, too, an invitation should not be addressed, "Mr. and Mrs. John Doe and Family." Each grown member of the family should receive a separate invitation. Children are not usually invited to a wedding, but if they are the *inner* envelope may be "Mr. and Mrs. Doe" and beneath, "Jane, John and Nancy."

An invitation to the church ceremony only does not require a reply. An invitation to the reception or to a home ceremony (here the reception is tacitly assumed) does require a reply —and a prompt one.

Announcements of a wedding are usually sent only if the wedding is a small one. Occasionally, however, they are sent to those at a distance or, in the case of a couple with a great many acquaintances, to all who did not receive wedding invitations. They should be addressed, sealed and stamped, ready for mailing so that they can be put in the mail as soon as possible after the wedding. The usual wording is:

> *Mr. and Mrs. John Henry Smith*
> *have the honour to announce*
> *the marriage of their daughter*
> *Mary Jane*
> *to*
> *Mr. Paul Peter Brown*
> *on Monday, the third of June*
> *One thousand nine hundred and sixty-four*
> *All Angels Church*
> *New York*

Although it is sufficient merely to give the date of the wedding, it is more gracious to also include the place.

A young woman who is married for the second time usually has her parents announce the marriage. In this case her name is given as "Mary Brown Smith." In the case of a more mature couple, they usually announce their own wedding.

Although an engraved announcement may be sent, a personal note or telephoned announcement is customary.

An elopement is usually announced in the same way as any other quiet wedding. The announcement should be made as soon as possible. In society circles, the simplest thing is to notify the society editor of the paper. Otherwise, an engraved announcement should be sent.

"At Home" cards may be sent with the invitations, but I don't approve of sending them with announcements since it seems like a bid for gifts. The usual form (without name) is

> *Will Be At Home*
> *After June Third*
> *Ten Pine Street*

If, after invitations have been sent out, the engagement is broken, the easiest way to notify friends and relatives is by telegram. If there is time, however, a printed card may be sent. No reason is given for a broken engagement, but if the marriage is postponed because of death or illness this is stated. If a printed card, rather than a telegram, is sent, this is the wording:

> *Mr. and Mrs. John Henry Smith*
> *Announce that the marriage of their daughter*
> *Mary Jane*
> *to*
> *Mr. George Doe*
> *will not take place*

Those invited to the wedding reception send gifts, addressed to the bride, before the wedding if possible. An invitation to the church only or an announcement does not require a gift, but of course it is always correct (and certainly gracious) to send one.

27

Mourning Etiquette

WE ALL, at some time, lose a family member, relative or friend. Although it is not feasible to give etiquette rules for those immediately concerned, it is advisable to have some information about the various problems that arise when planning a funeral. This chapter, then, is intended as a general guide for those who stand by the bereaved family, as well as the mourners.

Although we rightly feel that we want to give our dead a fitting and respectful funeral, it is the obligation and duty of the one who talks with the undertaker, discusses and makes the final arrangements to keep the cost within the means of the bereaved family. For this reason, it is advisable, if possible, for the family to call on a relative or trusted friend to help with such details. All too often, the man or woman who has suffered the personal loss is too stunned, too overwhelmed to take a calm practical attitude toward the selection of a casket and various interment suggestions (all of which may increase the bill) that a funeral director may make.

As soon as the doctor has issued a death certificate and the funeral director has been called, the members of the family should make a list of those who must be notified. Where possible, this should be done by telephone, with the calls made by a relative or intimate friend. Telegrams should be sent only as a last resort—especially to those who were close to the deceased.

Although the funeral director is willing to take care of the wording of an obituary notice, it is advisable to have a member of the family (here, again, that devoted close friend can be helpful) check the wording. Too often a married daughter or sister is listed as "*Mrs.* Mary Jones," which is incorrect. She should be "Mary Smith Jones."

Although flowers are usually sent, many people today prefer no flowers or to have them from the immediate family only. In this case, it is customary to make some suggestions regarding a substitute. The usual form is a last line in the death notice, "In lieu of flowers, please send donations to The Heart Fund." Most funds of this kind—the Cancer Committee, March of Dimes and so on—welcome such donations and send a memorial card noting the contribution, though not the amount, to the family of the deceased. Although large, well-known funds are usually designated, this is not obligatory and a family can suggest that the donation in memory of their loved one be made to a local church or orphanage. Sometimes the request is for aid to a research unit working on the condition that caused the death, sometimes it is to the deceased's favorite charity. It is not considered good form to add "Kindly omit flowers," but the line "Masses appreciated" or "In lieu of flowers, please donate to your favorite charity" may be added. It is well to remember that in some religions, namely the Jewish, flowers are not sent. It is advisable, therefore, to check with funeral director or other source if in doubt about the religious views of the deceased or family.

Although many families of various faiths do not have the deceased lying in state or placed in an open casket, others assume that friends will want to view the body and make arrangements accordingly. For those who pay their respects in this way, there are a few governing rules. Upon entering the room it is customary to go directly to the casket. Roman Catholics kneel and say a short prayer, others stand quietly with bowed head. At a Catholic funeral there is usually a stand near the casket on which mass cards may be placed. (These are sympathy or memorial cards stating that a mass (or masses) has been requested by. . . .)

In funeral homes, most chapels or rooms in which caskets are placed have a book near the entrance in which those who paid their respects are expected to sign their names.

When one sees a member of the bereaved family, it is correct to clasp his hand and say, "Please accept my sympathy" or "You have my deepest sympathy." In the case of an intimate friend, it is a gracious gesture to add, "Please let me know if I can be of any help."

Bear in mind that most funeral chapels close at ten o'clock, which is a good policy, since otherwise a family can be exhausted if the various members remain there most of the time.

Since more and more church funerals are held every year, it seems advisable to offer a few suggestions. The processional forms in the rear or vestibule of the church where the clergyman meets the pallbearers bearing the casket. The clergyman is followed by the choir, then honorary pallbearers (if there are such), then the pallbearers with the casket. The family walks next, in pairs, the chief mourners first and if possible each woman accompanied by a man. The rest of the mourners follow in the order suggested by the funeral director, with the nearest and eldest relatives first. It is usual, if the chief mourner is a woman, for her to be accompanied by the one who will be the most help or comfort to her. For this and other personal reasons, it is often difficult or impossible to hold rigidly to the rule as to who follows whom, and relatives should not cause bickering or dissension about where they were placed or where they should have been placed at a funeral.

Whether a funeral is held from a funeral home with services at church or—unusual now but still correct—the funeral is conducted in the home, the funeral director at a given time will ask friends to "view the deceased." Friends then take a final look at the body, then relatives go to the casket; the last ones to do so are the chief mourners. After viewing the body, each group leaves the room. The funeral director then closes the casket.

Whether the service is held at home or in church, only the family members, relatives and most intimate friends go to the cemetery. Business associates and casual friends leave after the service.

There are no special etiquette rules regarding cremation. The funeral director can explain the details and the arrangements and customs in the crematory selected. Since some religions do not approve of it, the family must settle this with their church if it is planned to follow a church service with a cremation.

Formal mourning is seldom practiced nowadays. Naturally, the family members, chief mourners and close relatives wear black or dark colors at the funeral. Common sense dictates that, for the immediate family, bright colors, extreme styles and a great deal of jewelry are out of place for a few weeks or months. But solid, unrelieved black is seldom seen. It might be well to remember that respect for the dead is not all outward display. It is possible to dress as usual and still remember the beloved dead with private prayer and good works. Anything that helps make our corner of the world a better place might be a private memorial to the one we loved and lost. I admit it is poor taste for anyone to go to a dance or a very sophisticated show a week after a parent's death. But, on the other hand, attendance at the movies, a concert, a simple home party six or eight weeks later cannot be construed as lack of respect.

Mourning armbands are still seen in some parts of Europe but are no longer worn here. So, too, in this country, a child up until the age of fifteen or sixteen never wears any form of mourning—even at the funeral of a parent. Obviously, the attire is subdued.

The letters of thanks sent out by the bereaved family should be handwritten. It is not necessary for the chief mourner to actually write them, but they should go out in his name. A relative or close friend may write and sign the chief mourner's name to the notes that should be sent to all who sent flowers, mass or spiritual bouquet cards, or contributions to charity in the name of the deceased. These letters should be short, should mention "your beautiful flowers" or "the mass offering" or "John's favorite charity" and express appreciation.

Engraved cards of thanks are sent out only in the case of those who were very prominent. But even then such cards are sent to officials, professional or business associates, and those of the general public who sent flowers or telegrams. Such acknowledgment cards do not relieve the family of the obligation to send personal thank-you letters to their own friends.

28

The Teen Age

FROM THE RITES of passage let us now return to one of the
more general problems of modern manners which is nevertheless still not primarily involved with considerations of our own
social or business standing. It is true that to some extent
parents are judged by their children's behavior. Such judgments often reflect an accurate awareness of just how responsible parents are in this matter. But the social problems
of children and, more especially, of teenagers are so important in themselves, so agonizing and confusing to the young
people involved, that the way they affect the reputations of
parents must necessarily be given a lower priority. Our first
concern must plainly be with the happiness, welfare and
character-development of our children. And that is the view-
point from which this all-too-brief chapter must be read.

At present too much is said and written about "the teens."
Yet it is possible that our grandparents were right in their
division of the social ages. They considered all under sixteen

"children"—"young" and "older" but still collectively "children." From sixteen to twenty-one was the "young adult" period, and after twenty-one one was "adult."

Now we allot a very short time to childhood, then speak of the "pre-teens," "the teen age" and apparently consider teens over sixteen or seventeen as "grownup." The result? We have too many twelve-year-olds who ape their grown sisters, too many little girls who frequent beauty salons, too many pathetically sophisticated little creatures. They are forced into high school-age situations before they are old enough to cope with them. The same is true of boys, only to a lesser degree. Boys don't want to imitate their elders until they are at least fourteen. Girls seem to start acting like teenagers when they are little over ten or eleven.

Since this chapter is intended to cover the youngster in the period between childhood and maturity, we'll speak of the thirteen-to-seventeen-year-old "teen." After the eighteenth birthday the average boy or girl is a young adult and should be treated accordingly.

If I were asked to give one piece of advice to the parents of youngsters in this "teen group" I would say "Don't pry but always be ready to listen." At this age the child doesn't need the parent in the physical sense, and too often the parents pay little attention to the emotional or mental needs of this group. On the other hand, this is the age of conformity— which in many cases takes strange forms from an adult's point of view. This is the time when all boys want their hair cut the same, all girls want the same kind of clothes, same hairdo, same nail polish.

Since the adolescent battle cry "Everybody does it" will be heard in every home, it is well for the parents of a young "teenager" to decide early on "ground rules," curfew hours, allowances, all the do's and don'ts that can come up—and then *hold the line*. Obviously a fourteen-year-old girl should have more privileges than she had at twelve. But let's not forget that she is only fourteen and should be treated accordingly.

Possibly one of the first rules to settle is the time at which a youngster is expected home. Once this is established other standards should be fixed.

Friendships, parties, all the things that the others do are important to the teenager. Possibly one of the crucial events is the first party at home. Here understanding parents can be invaluable. The wise mother lets her son or daughter plan the menu (with as few suggestions as possible) and outline amusements. The party should be planned for a night when mother can be home to help but not be a part of the festivities. No matter what other parents may do, no matter what your offspring says about other youngsters' party arrangements, make up your mind that a party in your home will be chaperoned. Young people can't (and shouldn't) be left to themselves. Remember, though, your presence should be realized but not thrust on the young guests. Don't try to be "one of the group," because you are not, don't try to draw youngsters into conversation, and don't stay in the party room. Helping with the refreshments or the supper is a wonderful way to keep in touch with, but not seem a part of, your youngster's party. Obviously no liquor should be served at a party of this kind, and beer or liquor brought in must be forfeited by the wouldbe donor. Liquor that is opened on the sly should be confiscated at once. The party should end at a reasonable hour with no suggestion of the crowd going for hot dogs or for a ride to end the evening.

Teenage Etiquette: Advice to and about teenagers should primarily be addressed to them, so the following is a guide for the girl or boy who wants to be popular, wants to be poised, and wants to do the correct thing according to the standards of his group combined with accepted etiquette rules.

Graduation brings special problems. Here are condensed answers to many of them.

Today many high schools and junior high schools require graduates to wear academic gowns. If this is not the case and students are given an outline of what to wear, abide by the prescribed rules. If all girls wear street length dresses, the one who appears in a floor length gown is out of order. If boys wear blue or gray suits and white shirts, one shouldn't arrive in a blue or plaid shirt.

If you're invited to another's graduation party, a gift is in order. It is not necessary, however, to give gifts to all your classmates, nor is it necessary to give or send a gift if you receive a formal graduation invitation or announcement.

The class prom or senior dance is an important social event to the average teenager. If it is the girl's dance, she invites a boy and she pays for the tickets. If a boy asks a girl who is in his class, he obviously buys the tickets just as he would if she were not in his school. A girl should never ask a boy classmate to escort her to the dance. No matter how well she knows him, if he doesn't come through with an invitation she has no choice but to invite an "outside" boy.

Despite the teenage fad for staying out all night after the senior dance, it still remains a silly *juvenile* practice. If possible, ask the school authorities to extend the dance another hour. If this can't be managed, the members of the class and guests should all go to someone's home, or, in the case of a big school, various groups should repair to specified homes for bacon and eggs, coffee and buns, or other form of breakfast. Groups of boys and girls wandering around night clubs or driving along roads are a danger to themselves and can cause accidents. If your class can't agree on "after-the-dance" activities, let the night end when the dance ends (which is the more sensible course, anyway).

Teen time is "date time" and should be fun. However, the present tendency toward "going steady" and early engagements is another facet of the "too old too soon" problem mentioned earlier. A fourteen-year-old girl is not old enough for steady dating. A sixteen-year-old boy should not be confined to dating one girl. If you're sensible you won't tie yourself down too early, and if your parents are sensible they won't encourage the "boy friend" roles until you are old enough to make an adult choice.

It is not possible for an etiquette book to cover the subject of petting, romancing or call-it-what-you-will. But a word on "conduct in public" seems needed as never before. Whether yours is a casual date or an undying love, don't display it in public. The boy and girl who cling in a torrid embrace on a street corner are not romantic-looking figures. They look cheap and their conduct cheapens the love they flaunt.

Not only girls, but frequently boys, feel that they are not popular, that they are social duds. Although it is true that some of every generation will lack personality, charm, the ability to make friends, the chances are that most of the young people who feel left out are merely late bloomers. Not all the roses in the garden bloom at the same time. The bud that opens tomorrow may be just as beautiful as the one that bloomed today. So, too, the girl who is quiet and timid at fourteen may well be a real beauty at twenty. The boy who is shy and ill at ease at sixteen may find himself in college or in his first job. Teenage popularity is an indefinite thing, and although it is pleasant to be liked by one's contemporaries, remember, you may be a "late bloomer" so don't worry about it.

29

*The Unmarried
Man and Woman*

PRECEPTS THAT COME under the heading of etiquette are too often directed exclusively toward the girl who lives at home, and scant attention is given to the girl in a studio apartment or apartment hotel. Yet the girl who has the conventional background of home life, family and friends is not nearly so much in need of counsel as the girl "on her own"—whether twenty or bordering forty. And if the bachelor girl is neglected, what of that character dear to fiction writers of a past generation, the man who lives in a club hotel or has a small apartment. This chapter is especially for those who are many times "alone in a crowd."

It would be rash to tell the twenty-year-old stenographer that she must have a chaperon accompany her when she goes to the annual dance of the organization that employs her. It would also be rash to tell the girl who earns a fairly good salary in a semi-executive position that she must hire a chaperon to live with her, since she is only twenty-seven.

As for the young business man who decides to "throw" a cocktail party for his co-workers, he is certainly not going to get a chaperon to help him entertain the girls who spend eight hours a day working with him. The rules laid down for the girl who dwells at home, for the society man who entertains in his bachelor apartment, for the girl whose life is a round of teas, dances, Junior League meetings and dates do not apply to the vast army of gainfully employed young people.

Let's begin at the very beginning of a girl's business career. If she arrives in a strange city, she'll wisely register at a woman's hotel or a club residence. This is much better than taking an apartment immediately. For one thing, it gives her an opportunity to find out what neighborhood will be most convenient for her in future, and it also means that she won't foolishly sign a lease on an apartment in an undesirable house. One takes enough chances on one's neighbors in any city, without moving into a house that is noted for the character (or lack of it) of its tenants. Although some will argue that the house a man lives in is not so important, I think the above suggestion is a good one for young men to follow also.

Unless one has brought notes of introduction, social contacts in a city must be made through those with whom one works, through residents of the house in which one lives, through such social agencies as the "Y," or through the church one attends. But don't expect much social help from city churches; the congregations are largely transient, and often so large that it is impossible for their clergymen to meet and know them all.

My first suggestion regarding social contacts that are established during office hours is: Go slow. This is especially true of girls. And don't think that the girls in the office are jealous if they warn you not to notice a certain handsome salesman. Jealousy may play a part, but it has been known that a green little typist ignored what a head stenographer meant for very good motherly advice—and later regretted it.

Very often young men do not want the responsibility of an apartment and continue to live in a hotel or club room year after year. Less often girls feel the same way. Well, for those who like it, this is a good and economical way to live.

If, however, the question of taking an apartment comes up, weigh all the points involved carefully. To begin with, do you like being alone? Do you want to keep house? Do you want to live by yourself, or share the apartment with one or two others?

You decide to share an apartment? Well and good. This has both advantages and disadvantages. You'll have companionship, you'll be able to share your guests, and (if you're a girl) it won't be awkward to have one of the opposite sex visit you. Your friend, possibly sound asleep in her own room, may with all propriety be considered a chaperon.

Now for the disadvantages. You'll have to adjust yourself to some extent to the other person. If you share a two-room apartment, and you like to type late at night, a roommate who retires at ten may not consider you a joy. Of two people living together, one is very apt to be steady, while the other slides out of responsibility and is thoughtless to the last degree. One likes to cook, the other doesn't. One abhors untidiness, the other hates the process of cleaning house. The clothes-borrowing proclivity of some girls is another case in point. It isn't a bit funny to rush home from the office, all thoughts centered on wearing your new chiffon dress, and discover that your roommate had a date and borrowed it! Yet this happens time and again. These are some of the small trials of sharing an apartment. There are bigger ones.

I know a man whose roommate left his ties and socks alone —but calmly took his best girl away from him!

Where two girls share a one-room apartment, they have to be even more congenial. If one wants to entertain a date in the room, the other must diplomatically take herself to a movie or get invited out for the evening. Cooperation and consideration are the only solutions. Otherwise a very popular girl who lives with a bespectacled, retired friend may make her roommate's life miserable by expecting the poor girl to spend four or five nights each week at the local movies or in the bathroom or kitchenette!

There are the financial arrangements to be considered. The girl who takes an apartment and installs all the necessary equipment for housekeeping without first working out a practical budget is both courageous and inexperienced. And by "budget" I mean just that! The girl or man alone in a big city must consider not only the day-to-day expenses but the possible emergencies as well. As far as rent is concerned, the rule of thumb is not to pay more than 25 per cent of one's net income in this category. Exceptions to this rule should be rare. That's the first item in a rough budget. Then you must think of food, clothing, insurance, transportation, medical expenses, repairs and cleaning, a Christmas and vacation savings account, entertainment and incidentals.

I don't know why, but people have a quaint way of being less considerate of the friends who live in "bachelor quarters" than of those who live at home. Few people nowadays drop in unexpectedly on a family, but it's taken for granted by many otherwise quite well bred men and women that they may "run in to see Jack" at any hour. The dweller in a one-room apartment is sometimes sorely tempted to be rude to a Sunday-morning caller or a college classmate who "drops in" near midnight. After all, single men and women have to earn a living, and they are not always in the mood to serve cocktails and be gaily entertaining.

Buffet suppers, Sunday-night cocktail parties and informal weekend brunches are the usual methods of entertaining on small means and in limited space. Of course, the girl who wants to show her best date how gratifyingly domestic she is at heart may invite him to her apartment for dinner. The first time this is attempted, however, I'd suggest making it a dinner of four.

I maintain that the girl who lives alone has a real problem on her hands, for she must be sure her associates understand that it is "freedom" she seeks and not "free love." Many men have to be convinced of this distinction, unfortunate as the fact may be. Even the chap whose life is an open book occasionally tries to see how far he'll get with strictly dishonorable intentions! Susan, who dwells safely within parental walls, may ask a date to come in when he escorts her home from the movies and no one will give it a second thought, But let Sally bring a man into her tiny apartment two minutes after midnight—all of her neighbors suddenly become interested! I'd say "Ignore the neighbors," but the worst of it is that the man involved may also get the wrong idea.

Even though it is comparatively early, you should always be sure of the men you take into your apartment. It's always silly to ask in casual strangers. But it would be carrying the conventions to the nth degree if you didn't invite a home-town boy who is in your city for a few hours between trains to come up for a drink.

Regarding where you'll go and with whom you'll go, all anyone can advise is that you use your common sense and don't forget that, even though a silly escapade may be harmless enough, there's nothing gained by getting a reputation for being reckless.

The wealthy bachelor who has a well-staffed household can and should give dinner parties and entertain those in whose homes he is a visitor. Naturally, if he has young women guests, he'll have some older woman present. The business man in moderate circumstances should confine his entertaining to less elaborate parties. There's no reason in the world why a young man may not invite his fiancee and another couple for dinner at his apartment. In a metropolitan city a man who knows a girl well may, with all propriety, invite her alone to his apartment. But this is one of those conventions that may be accepted in a big city while they are frowned on in a small town.

In society circles, the single man or woman who maintains an apartment is expected to repay social obligations in the usual manner: by giving luncheons, dinners or cocktail parties. The business man or woman is excused from this. But, for this reason, the man who is a frequent dinner guest at a married friend's home should occasionally take candy or flowers to his hostess. The single girl who cannot return the hospitality of a married friend should send a small gift, take her hostess to lunch in a hotel, or suggest a matinee some afternoon. In other words, if you don't repay your social obligations in the usual way, do so in a way more in keeping with your manner of living.

This brings us to a consideration of those shifting distinctions between a life of propriety in a small town and a life of comparable propriety in a city.

In a city it is not nearly so important that one be circumspect. For instance, among young business people in New York or Chicago it is taken for granted that a girl will ask a man to her apartment or that the man who has his own rooms will invite a girl for Sunday breakfast or a before-dinner cocktail. In matters such as this, one must be guided by a mixture of common sense and a knowledge of the conventions of the place and one's associates.

In any large city a great deal of business (and I don't mean "monkey business") is transacted over a meal or cocktail. No one would talk unpleasantly of a married attorney who took a woman client to lunch, or about any young business man who on his way home stopped for a cocktail with one of his feminine co-workers. But here, too, common sense must be used. It's all right to be seen in public with a married business associate, but the man or woman who lives alone should consider carefully before inviting the married one home.

Despite the long-accepted theory that in a large city one is swallowed up, a tiny cog in a vast machine, I've found that any large city is made up of sections—and each section is a small town, with its small-town characters, gossip and grapevine telegraph. You may not know him, he may not know your exact name, but the elderly man who daily walks out of the apartment across the street just as you start to the subway may well be aware of the fact that when you lived six blocks away one of your inebriated guests kicked in the front door—and cost you a dispossess.

"What then," you ask, "is the difference between New York and Four Corners?" Just this: In Four Corners, you'd know your neighbor and know he knew your business; in New York or Chicago or San Francisco, you don't know *him* but he knows a little about you. This is one other reason for knowing your neighborhoods before taking an apartment.

30

The Divorcée

IN GRANDMOTHER'S DAY a divorce was considered a stain on the family escutcheon. The divorcée took her place in the closet reserved for family skeletons, and was spoken of in the muted tone used for all sad or shady objects. In those days a family friend had to make a definite choice between Mary and Jack. If, after the divorce or separation, she welcomed Mary into her home, the door of her house was closed forever to Mary's former husband. It was unthinkable for a divorced couple to meet socially. Now, in many circles, it is not at all unusual for Jack to be invited to dinner to meet Mary's second husband.

If a previous generation frowned upon divorce, there is still no reason to smile on it today. It almost inevitably leaves painful and unsightly scars. But there are times when it is the necessary and only happy, satisfactory solution. Whether it is accepted as a boon or a catastrophe, it should be treated with dignity, and the couple who decide upon a divorce, after giving the subject every consideration, should do all possible to maintain mutual respect. An open hearing in which charges and countercharges, recriminations and family scandals are freely aired may provide some spicy journalistic fare, some intriguing reading for the curious public, and some fat legal fees—but it also exposes two adults shorn of dignity, self-restraint and all the essentials of good breeding. The dignified divorce may be a solution to one's marital problems. The sensational one is an affront to good taste.

If it is silly to speak unkindly about a former fiancé, it is even more absurd to speak disparagingly about a former spouse. After all, if you married a man who was dull, untidy and boorish, it was nothing to your credit. If it took you eleven years to find out that Jack was your inferior, you can't expect your friends to laud you as a good judge of character!

After the divorce, the less said about your matrimonial upset the better. This will be a kindness to yourself and to your friends, but more than that, it is a kindness that parents owe to the children who may be involved. It is hard enough on a child to have to spend six months of every year with each parent, or to live with Mother but have a stiff and formal visit from Daddy once a week. But when the child constantly hears his parents criticizing each other, he's bound either to become callous and cynical toward both or to favor one. In either case, he's bewildered, unhappy and unsettled —and loses his sense of security. Few adults realize just what a feeling of security means to a child. And every youngster is entitled to it.

All classes of mortals have their particular problems, but the divorcée's lot is among the hardest. This is especially true of the young girl. Many men, even the very nice ones, seem to think that a girl who is divorced or separated from her husband is fair game. It's bad enough if the divorcée lives with her family, but if she elects to live alone she must be prepared to set all new masculine acquaintances straight regarding her mode of living. For this reason, I think that the young girl who obtains a divorce will do well to have a friend or relative live with her, at least for the first period of her new life.

The divorcée must realize that unless she lives in a large city she'll be freely discussed by her neighbors and each trivial thing she does will be considered and analyzed from every angle. A young widow will receive sympathy, but a young divorcée in the average small community is every woman's enemy until she proves herself otherwise. With this in mind, the recently divorced girl should be circumspect. Fighting for one's virtue is hard, but having to convince everyone that that virtue is intact is an awful bore!

The divorced woman, whether she is young or not, keeps her engagement ring and any other jewelry that she has received from her husband. She keeps her wedding ring, too, but doesn't wear it. If she has an independent income (and a bit of pride) she doesn't accept alimony. Ordinarily, the couple divide their worldly possessions, although in most instances the wife receives the bulk of the household effects.

Despite the fact that she doesn't have to change her name, the average divorcée prefers to change it. The only reason for this is convenience. It would create an embarrassing situation if John Green Rich were to remarry and the two Mesdames John Green Rich were to live in the same neighborhood! But the divorcée, like her sorrowing sister, the widow, should not use her Christian or first name as part of her social title. If the combination of her maiden name and her married name is euphonious, she wisely adopts it. For instance, when Mary Jane Brown marries and later divorces John Green Rich, she is thereafter known as Mrs. Brown Rich or Mrs. M. Brown Rich. She does *not* have Mrs. Mary Rich engraved on her stationery.

Very often the divorcée obtains permission to resume her maiden name. If there are no children, this is ideal—but children complicate the situation. For instance, an adolescent Jane Rich will be constantly—and perhaps at some pain or embarrassment to herself—explaining to her friends and associates that her mother, Miss Mary Brown, was formerly Mrs. Rich. Needless to say, the divorcée who is known as Miss should be Miss Maiden Name. She can't go under the name of Miss and continue to use her former husband's name, for she was never Miss Married Name.

The question of the name is one that each divorcée must decide for herself—always bearing in mind that her name should be chosen with a thought to euphony, her own dignity and the future of any children involved.

The wise course for friends of a couple who reach a parting of the ways is to say nothing. If Mary tells you anything about Jack, refrain from comment—and don't repeat her confidence. Very often one of the parties in a divorce will want to talk to someone. But the person who talks is very apt to regret it later. For that reason the recipient of a confidence should say as little as possible. Or the couple may reconsider and have a reconciliation. If they do, any unkind truths that have been told to you are best completely forgotten—or at least never mentioned.

Although divorce is now so common, not all families treat it in the casual way of some of our moderns. Therefore the wise hostess runs no risks with her divorced friends! Possibly young Pat Carney and his former wife parted on friendly terms and won't mind meeting casually at your dinner table.

On the other hand, Mrs. Staid Fifty may have been heart-broken about the divorce that she allowed her graying husband so that he might marry a twenty-year-old actress. It would be cruel, thoughtless and stupid to bring them together at a dinner. The safe rule to follow is: Don't invite them unless you're sure of their reactions. Even if you think you're sure, consider the possibilities carefully. These stories of estranged couples who are still "good friends" should always be taken with a grain of salt, for, frankly, the friendly divorce is the exception rather than the rule. One party concerned may bear no ill-will toward the other, but it's extremely hard to find a divorced couple still "good friends" in the true sense of the term. Possibly in one case out of ten neither party will feel wronged or unhappy about a parting. In the other nine cases, "good friends" simply means that they won't come to blows on sight! If there remains in one or the other a flame of resentment, a feeling of having been wronged or cheated, or—saddest of all—a little spark of marital devotion, that one is bound to prefer not to see or hear about the former matrimonial partner.

If you're certain of your divorced friends and bring them together under your roof, make no apologies or explanations. You'll use tact and not insist on introducing Julie's new husband to her discarded one—but on the other hand you'll refrain from comment if you see Julie talking to her former husband or in deep conversation with his bride.

Briefly, friends of divorced couples have an important mission. By keeping silent when silence is due and by saying the tactful and true thing when speech is necessary, they are of inestimable help in preserving that dignity which is the cornerstone of a decent divorce.

31

Travel Etiquette

As SOON AS one decides to "go"—whether on a cruise to Bermuda, a plane trip to Europe, or a bus trip half way across the country—the first question that occurs is "what clothes shall I take" or, for better planning, "What clothes will I actually need"!

What any traveler will need must depend on destination, way of life, method of travel, and activities on arrival. The most important thing to remember when packing is "The less luggage the better." Every extra piece of luggage presents an added disadvantage. In addition to the worry of losing bags is the very definite problem, almost as prevalent in Europe as here, caused by a shortage of porters. This is the reason for the great popularity of "airplane" or other especially lightweight luggage. Oh, good matched leather luggage looks impressive, but it can be frightening to survey three or four such bags when there is not a porter in sight!

Trunks, by the way, are seldom used nowadays—unless when transporting all one's family and family goods.

In packing, one must decide what clothes are to be frequently used during the trip, what can be left packed for a great part of the time. A small train case or overnight case is a "must" for toilet requirements, a sleeping garment, slippers, possibly a blouse or (for a man) shirt and tie. This permits freshening up while traveling, or a slight wardrobe variation after an overnight stay, and yet the main luggage may be left undisturbed.

Let us first consider travel by ship. At this point a word to those who "see the travelers off" seems timely. A friend should arrive an hour before departure time and leave well in advance of the "All ashore" signal, since family members should have a few minutes alone with the travelers. Bon Voyage gifts are sometimes a distinct problem. A small growing plant can give as much pleasure as a big bunch of cut flowers—and not take up as much room. If the travelers really like fruit, a huge basket may be a joy, but bear in mind that such baskets were originally sent when it was difficult to obtain fruit or delicacies aboard ship. Nowadays most ships are floating hotels, and modern refrigeration allows for the storage of fruits and the like so the average traveler, whether first class or tourist, hardly needs extra foods or goodies. Large, bulky packages or gifts of wearing apparel should be sent to the voyager's home well before departure time. Small gifts, whether fruits, flowers, plants, liquor, candy or books, may be sent to the ship.

The Chief Steward should be consulted about dining salon seating arrangements. If there are two seatings, this should be settled and also whether the passenger will be at a small table or a slightly larger one. Unless a group requests otherwise, most tables are for two or four, with a few for eight.

The deck steward is the one to see about a deck chair, where it is to be placed and so on.

Good manners on a boat are no different from good manners elsewhere. A passenger should not monopolize game tables, deck games or the TV set in the lounge. It goes without saying that loud talking, laughter and singing in or near cabins is out of order—especially at night.

Shipboard friendships do not obligate us to continue the friendship, exchange home addresses and so on. Of course this may be and often is done. But a well-bred traveler avoids pushing or forcing himself on others and certainly avoids too-friendly overtures from slight acquaintances.

All guests who breakfast in the dining salon should be fully dressed. Night clothes and a robe are sufficient attire when the steward brings a tray to the cabin, however.

For day wear the average woman passenger chooses simple suits, dresses, skirt-and-sweater combinations or sports attire. Shorts and slacks may be worn in the dining salon at breakfast but at no other meals. In tourist class it is possible to get along with a formal afternoon dress for gala dinners and a more simple one or a typical daytime dress for others. Hats are never obligatory and seldom worn but are, of course, correct at lunch. A man wears a business suit, or sport clothes, or slacks and a blazer. Both men and women need some form of coat, regardless of the season in which they travel.

The passenger in first class usually has more changes of clothes and wears a more dressy dress at average dinners, an evening or dinner dress for gala nights. She wears a dinner dress and her best accessories if she is put at the captain's table, and wears an evening dress or formal dinner dress if invited to the captain's dinner. A gentleman wears a dinner jacket at dinner if he always dresses at home but may, if he prefers, wear a dark business suit. The dinner jacket is a "must" in conservative circles if he attends the captain's dinner, and for the ship's concert or crew's show. His day wear is about the same as that suggested for tourist travel.

On most ships, there is a captain's dinner for specially invited guests in first class, and a captain's Cocktail Party for special tourist class guests. Naturally, for each class, these are the most formal occasions of the trip and passengers invited dress accordingly.

A passenger who requires the services of the doctor during the trip should give him a gift (a monetary one will do) since, although paid by the owners of the boat, he likes to think his help is appreciated.

So many employees do so much for the passengers that it is hard to know just whom to tip, yet their tips are an important part of their income from their work. (Nobody ever took a job as steward, matron or clerk aboard a ship for the basic salary.) At some convenient time toward the end of the trip tips should be given to the cabin and deck stewards; the dining salon steward is tipped at the last or next-to-last meal. The library steward is tipped if his services have been used, and this is also true of other stewards and stewardesses. The amount of each tip will, of course, depend on the way in which the passenger travels, the services rendered and the attitude during the voyage. (It is usual to tip bar stewards and employees in beauty or barber salons at the time of service.) The average tourist-class passenger might allow twenty-five to thirty dollars for tips. The passenger in first class should up this to fifty dollars or more, always depending on service requested and how given.

A cruise usually offers all the advantages of an ocean voyage at less cost. For this reason cruises are popular with young people. For the most part etiquette rules are the same as those suggested for ship travel. The tips, too, should be figured about the same way, although for a five-day cruise it is possible for a tourist-class passenger to get by with twenty dollars for tips.

Young women should be especially circumspect about making friends on a cruise. Oh, they may dance and have fun while it lasts, but should not be too quick to invite men to call on them at home, should not assume too much. Since the cruise is strictly a pleasure trip, sport clothes are worn all day, evening clothes from dinner time on.

Train travel, although sometimes more difficult, does not have as many obligations for the passenger as boat travel. Obviously a long trip in a day coach can be an ordeal. A trip in a roomette, however, can be pleasant and relaxing. Unless ill or infirm, a passenger should not remain in the roomette all through the trip if it is a long one. He should vary things with a trip to the observation car, to the club car for refreshments (they can, of course, be served in the roomette, but I'm suggesting "change of scenery"), and to the dining car for meals.

Arrived at the dining car, he writes his order on the pad supplied for the purpose. It is permissible to ask the steward (waiter) for suggestions, but he does not take verbal orders. If, as often happens, strangers are put at the same table, they may converse, but there is no obligation to exchange home addresses and the like. The dining car steward is tipped according to the bill for the meal—roughly 15 to 20 percent of the amount.

Car porters and stewards who serve during the trip should be tipped accordingly. Fifty cents is an average for a short day trip, a dollar for a longer one. An overnight trip minimum tip would, of course, be a dollar per night, more according to service rendered.

One who travels with children should remember that the youngsters are not the responsibility of the employees or other passengers. Toys or books should be taken along for the amusement of the children, and their traveling companion must face the fact that other passengers should not be disturbed or inconvenienced by whining or squabbling youngsters. Everyone has sympathy for the woman traveling with an infant, but run-about children who explore the car, run screaming through corridors, and in general make undue noise are the fault of the adult with them.

When traveling by air, remember that the weight of luggage per passenger is restricted. Possibly this form of travel, more than any other one thing, has made us experts on looking well dressed with a minimum of luggage. The seasoned traveler keeps an overnight or train case with him for use on the plane. Women who wear high-heeled or extreme shoes may want to put a pair of comfortable slippers in the case they hold on the plane. In it also might be toilet requirements and reading material. Luggage is weighed and excess charged for at the airport. The co-pilot sees that all luggage is safely stored away on the plane before passengers board it. Tickets are collected in the office, passengers follow the passenger agent or a co-pilot out to the plane on the runway.

Passengers adjust their seat straps when so instructed, do not loosen them until the order is given. So, too, they obey orders regarding when smoking is permitted and, in general, comply with all regulations. Although a few passengers hold spirited conversations, for the most part there is no attempt at really becoming acquainted. The attitude is similar to travel on a train—polite but desultory conversation or reading usually takes up the time. On long flights refreshments and food seem (to me, at least) to be served continuously. No sooner is "supper" finished on a night flight to Dublin or London than the smiling stewardesses start distributing before-breakfast fruit juices!

Co-pilots will answer questions. Stewardesses are glad to do all possible for the comfort of passengers, but all air lines prohibit passengers speaking to the pilot. All rules, all requests made by the stewardess on duty should be graciously accepted. Since stewardesses and co-pilots are considered "professionals," they are *not* tipped.

When traveling by automobile, we should make every effort to show courtesy to other drivers, consideration toward those in restaurants, inns or motels where we stop. The wise driver gets off the road in the late afternoon and selects his overnight stop accordingly. In very rural sections such signs as "Tourist Accommodations" and "Guests" are the indications that overnight patrons are welcome. In more traveled sections, along thruways and state roads, motels and tourist cabins dot the highway. There are no rules other than those of ordinary courtesy to guide one in the former small places, but the standard hotel rules regarding registering and tips to employees prevail in the larger, hotel-like places. Even if all wear shorts or slacks while on the road, it is wise to have a change of clothes, such as a simple dress or skirt for a woman, and a white shirt, fresh slacks and jacket for a man—in case the travelers decide to go to a good restaurant or spend the night in a resort hotel. One easily gotten-at "dress" outfit for each member of the group is also important for those who want to go to a church if traveling on Sunday. The considerate car traveler realizes that other overnight guests in the house may want to rise and leave early so he avoids loud talk, laughter or unnecessary noises late at night.

Bus trips differ little from car trips. Comfortable noncrushable clothes are preferred. The bus company or tour agent arranges stops, so passengers have no special obligations, other than tips, on such a trip.

When traveling, if possible make your hotel reservations

in advance. It is not always feasible, of course, but it saves time and embarrassment when it can be done. Arriving guests are met by a porter or bellman who takes the luggage, leads the way and indicates the desk. When registering, a man alone signs "John Smith—Pine Street, New York." When accompanied by his wife, he signs "Mr. and Mrs. . . ." and when children are along, he enters their names, not using such expressions as "and children" or "and family." A woman alone prefixes her name with the title "Miss" or "Mrs." An American plan hotel charges by day or week and the charge includes all meals or, recently, breakfast and dinner. A European plan hotel charges for room only and guests may either pay when served meals or sign the tab, and the amount for meals eaten is added to the bill at the end of the stay. Obviously the European plan works out best for travelers, since one is then free to explore local dining places.

In small hotels most guests talk and become chummy. This is particularly true of American-plan resort hotels. In large ("commercial" or "transient") hotels this is seldom the case.

It is correct for a guest to read while waiting for service in a hotel dining room. The exception would be if he shares a table with another guest. In this case it is considered impolite to "hide behind a book."

The advent of no-iron and drip-dry clothes of every description has eliminated much of the bother of travel and cut out the need for a great deal of luggage. Before starting a trip the wise traveler checks up on all such time- and work-saving helps. Having cut his luggage requirements to a minimum, eliminated all but necessary items from his wardrobe, he is ready to travel—better equipped but less baggage-laden than ever before.

32

"When in Rome"

THE MEMBERS OF the "international" set or the "jet" set have no need for advice on getting along with those in other countries. They are as much at home in Rome as in New York and can be equally enthusiastic about a Park Avenue cooperative and transforming an old French mill into a house.

Most of us, however, find foreign travel more challenging than that. Whether you are on a business assignment and know that the impression you make will have an effect on your negotiations, or you are simply traveling for pleasure but are conscious of your responsibility as an "ambassador of good will," the problem of how to behave when abroad will be a real one.

Many large international corporations, as well as the Foreign Service and overseas military commands, provide their people with more or less elaborate printed information on behavioral requirements in foreign lands. Although many of these guides are excellent, their distribution and sometimes their applicability (as, for example, in the case of military courtesies) is limited. More often than not we are forced to fall back on some sort of improvisation based on what we know of the country we are visiting, what we know about manners in general, and common sense. It would be ideal if there were a brief set of universal rules that, if followed, would bring us successfully through any social situation we might encounter abroad. I should be less than honest if I said there were. But, as we shall see, there *is* one rule that no one has yet been able to improve upon.

The majority of travelers can be divided into two groups: those who travel but try to create their "own home town" in every country they visit, who feel that we should not adjust to the country but that the country should make the adjustments for us. The second group, almost more irritating to the resident of another country, is made up of those who determinedly try to out-French the French and out-Greek the Greek! They *know* all the customs, traditions, social taboos of whatever country they enter. They are not content with complying with local custom; they'll see to it that the natives comply, too.

Between these two extremes is the Golden Mean—the happy medium. If I were asked to give one all-embracing etiquette rule that would apply everywhere, I would answer "the Golden Rule." The visitor in a strange country can't go far wrong if he tries to do the kindly thing. Ideally, of course, he should first try to obtain a working knowledge of the customs and important etiquette rules.

We are, to a great extent, more casual than most Europeans. In addition, we are less quick to take offense at what we consider a social slight—and we are more practical. The average American farmer who stops his work, tinkers with your car, and repairs it sufficiently for you to drive to a gas station will not be offended if you try to reimburse him. He may not take the bill you offer him, but he won't deem the offer a blow to his pride, an insult or a form of degradation. The situation would be quite different, however, if the incident took place in Ireland.

It was in a small town in Ireland, too, that I discovered that it is good manners to leave the house keys in the lock "so that a wayfarer may enter if he has the mind to do so." The American students who rented a cottage and carefully "locked up" every night were considered "unfriendly clods" for so doing!

The visitor who has a letter of introduction to an Oriental should avoid taking a gift to him if he is invited to call. The Oriental will feel obligated to give a slightly better gift. A return visit—and another gift? It may be a family keepsake, it may be a cherished possession, but the Oriental will "mind his manners" and outdo the guest in the gift-giving ceremony.

In rural Holland and among the green farmlands of the Irish Free State the tourist who stops to admire the view or take some "native color" pictures may well be asked to enter the cottage for chocolate (Holland) or tea (Ireland). No matter how poor the occupants, they would be offended if offered money. "Hospitality is given from the heart" and cannot be bought, as any native would know. Amusingly, I discovered, however, that the tourist may later send a gift— and a monetary one will be welcome. So refreshments are offered with no strings attached and a gift is sent as a token of friendship—also with no strings attached.

It is not too difficult to ascertain the local customs in the area in which one travels. And if in doubt, fall back on the Golden Rule.

Moving to another community within the United States often poses problems similar to those met in foreign travel. The difference in manners between Sioux City and Tokyo may be greater than that between Sioux City and New York, but in spite of this (or maybe because of it) New Yorkers may not make as many allowances for what differences do exist as would the Japanese. This can be very trying if, for example, you have just been transferred by your company to the New York office and find, as is likely, that your initial socializing is company-connected. Obviously you have a considerable stake in impressing your new employers, colleagues and clients with your social presentability, but you find that certain things that you do or say, that you have always taken for granted as correct, seem to disconcert your new friends.

Comedies have been built around the smalltown visitor to a big city, jokes have been made about the provincial with his countrified manners, his narrow view. In many ways the big city dweller who goes to a small town is a form of reverse provincial. Actually this is true not only in a small town, for in a big city in which he is a newcomer he can be just as narrow, just as intolerant as his country counterpart.

The trite "When in Rome, do as the Romans do" should be taken seriously by all who for one reason or another move to a different community, whether the move be as simple as a change of borough or as drastic as a move across the country.

Basic manners are primarily the same in most sections of the United States and Canada. Kindliness and courtesy are a part of living in the West, just as in the East. But we must remember that each area of the country—in fact each city or suburban community—has its own customs, its traditional way of celebrating holidays, of entertaining. If we move to a new community, we must expect to adjust our social customs.

It is not possible to outline here the customs of various places in the United States, but the wise newcomer ascertains these customs and, unless he has some serious ethical reason for eschewing them, tries to adjust to his new social surroundings. As an example, a suave New York hostess would be astounded if her dinner guests arrived bearing a homemade cake, a huge box of cookies or candy, or a bottle of wine. Yet there are many sections of the country where the prospective dinner guest takes it for granted that a "gift" of this kind is in order. So, too, few city hostesses would think of issuing an invitation to "dessert," but in many smart suburban areas it is not unusual to do this or even to invite some guests to dinner, others to come for dessert and coffee only.

In most cities, when ladies wear dinner dresses their escorts wear dinner jackets. In suburbs, because husbands arrive from the city with barely time to wash up quickly before going out to dinner, the lady of the house is ready in a simple dinner dress. The hostess assumes that the distaff side will contribute the glamour and festive air to her party while the man—serene in mufti—takes it for granted that for him "dressing for dinner" is confined to more elaborate Saturday night parties.

Group parties to which the guests contribute part of the meal had their origin as church or parish gatherings, with each family arriving with a picnic supper. This type of party lends itself to the modern career girl's way of life in a small New York apartment. It is also not unusual to find young married couples "getting together" with each wife contributing a salad, rolls, meat or dessert for the buffet table. Indeed many professional couples in big cities are adapting the "ladies dress, escorts do not" practice for weekday dinners. Obviously this will never be a standard custom in very formal groups, but since such groups are in the minority, the practice may soon be as usual in the city as the suburb. One thing must be born in mind, however: when ladies wear even the most simple dinner dresses, their escorts should wear dark (navy or gray or black) suits, white shirts and conservative ties. So, we see that, far from always being trailblazers, city dwellers sometimes adapt a country or suburban custom that fits into their way of life.

In small towns and suburban and rural areas it is customary for neighbors to stop at the door and welcome newcomers, offering suggestions about local shops, services and professional and school information. In addition, the nearest neighbor often invites the new arrivals to her home for coffee or even asks them for dinner on their first day or before they are settled and unpacked. In a big city apartment this is not "ruled out," but it is very seldom done. In fact a simple "good morning" is considered sufficient recognition for one's neighbor, and most city dwellers would hesitate to either extend or accept an invitation in this casual manner. This does not mean that it is not possible to become acquainted with or even on friendly terms with an apartment neighbor. It *is* possible, but it is the exception, rather than the rule.

Just as the small town girl learns that she can't expect the warm friendliness of home in a huge impersonal apartment building, so the newcomer in any community must learn to adjust to his new surroundings. When we realize that formal etiquette rules can be made to fit our environment but basic good manners are changeless, we'll cease to be strangers in our new town.

33

Washington Etiquette

WHEN WE THINK of society in our nation's capital we associate it with officials, diplomats, all that goes to make Washington the exciting panorama that the citizenry imagines it to be. It is true, of course, that the White House and its occupants set the pace for the governmental social life. But this is only true to a small extent of the "Old Guard" in Washington. Actually there are two often mingling circles in the capital, just as New York has its mingling of "old society" and "cafe society" and Boston has an intellectual set that is separate but not apart from the Back Bay contingent.

Until the last few years "old society" went its way, adhering to staid social customs, conservative to the nth degree. But the official group, of which the White House is the hub, followed protocol to a nicety, avoided stepping on diplomatic toes (no small task, I assure you) and still managed, since the last World War, to make some phases of social life a little less formal and a lot more fun. In recent years the old Washington families are also "unbending."

Those who move in conservative Washington society circles need no advice about avoiding official blunders. But the transients, the varied groups that make up the official social set in each administration must watch out.

Many an inexperienced hostess has assumed that, since there would be some officials at her dinner, the State Department would arrange the seating for her. This is a mistake. The State Department is always glad to help, but it only arranges the seating for White House dinners. State dinners are given each season, such as the Cabinet, diplomatic, Supreme Court, Speaker's and the Vice President's dinners. Then there are the various dinners in honor of visiting dignitaries, and so on. The State Department does not claim to rule social activities other than those connected with the White House, but the employees will, purely as a courtesy, advise the puzzled hostess.

The following list is based on common sense and is intended only as a general guide. The hostess should bear in mind that, just as a private visitor in her home is given the preferred place, so a visiting dignitary is seated above a resident of equal rank—as a gracious gesture only. We must remember also that in seating officials the precedence is given to the rank, not the individual. Thus Mr. John Doe, as "His Excellency, the Ambassador" outranks a duke or prince who is a minor secretary in an embassy. We must bear in mind also that from time to time feuds have been stirred up in Washington social circles about the order of precedence. (The ladies always seem to be the ones who notice these things. An official's wife will wax indignant while he is completely unaware of any slight.)

1. Highest rank is given a visiting president or sovereign.
2. The President of the United States (the Vice President in his absence).

3. A cardinal or an ambassador on a special mission.

4. Foreign ambassadors, according to length of time in this country.

5. The Apostolic Delegate (he may precede the ambassadors).

6. The Chief Justice.

7. The Vice President (when the President is there).

8. The Speaker of The House.

9. Associate Justices of the Supreme Court.

10. Secretary of State.

At church gatherings the clergy outrank all secular officials, although they (churchmen) always give precedence to the President. At social gatherings cardinals are often ranked above all except the President. When any church official and secular official have equal rank, precedence is given to the clergyman.

The White House is always the center of social life in Washington, and all social events are planned with Presidential or White House activities in mind. The President and First Lady always try to make those invited to any function at the White House feel free to accept or decline. But who, regardless of his station in life, his political views, could consider an invitation to the White House as anything but a command? Such an invitation is always answered in the third person. The reply should be handwritten in ink, as follows:

Mr. and Mrs. John James Smith
have the honour to accept
the kind invitation of
The President and Mrs. Elected
for dinner on Monday the first of June
at eight o'clock

One who resides in Washington leaves or sends this "by hand" to the White House. In other cases it is sent through the mail.

Guests invited for eight o'clock arrive at about ten minutes before the hour. The Chief Usher and his assistants regulate everything, so the greenest novice has nothing to worry about. As gentlemen check their coats, each is given a card with a diagram of the table, his place indicated and directions as to whether he turns left or right as he enters the dining room. If ladies are present, this card also indicates the person he will take to dinner. The ushers see that all guests take their places in the room designated—usually the Blue Room—and ushers see that they stand according to rank, with highest rank nearest the door by which the President and First Lady will enter, preceded by the military and naval aides. The aides make the presentation of guests, one taking care of presenting to the President, the other aide presenting the guests to the First Lady. As they shake hands guests say "How do you do, Mr. President" and "How do you do, Mrs. Elected." After all guests have been presented one aide takes the ranking woman guest to the President, the other guides the ranking man guest to the First Lady. The band or an orchestra starts to play, the President and his dinner partner lead the way to the dining room, followed by the First Lady and her partner, then others, according to rank. The President and his wife sit down at once, since no one may sit while they are standing. Thus all may sit down when they find their places.

At official dinners ranking guests have only their titles on place cards, others have also their names. The following use rank only:

The President
The Vice President
The Archbishop of . . .
The . . . Ambassador
The . . . Minister
The Chief Justice
The Speaker
The Secretary of . . . (All Cabinet members)

It is impossible to achieve the informality of a private home in the White House, impossible to alter official dinners to any great extent. However, in recent administrations there have been changes. The Roosevelts were trail blazers in this regard. The Trumans made no attempt to socialize beyond "the call of duty." The late President Kennedy and Mrs. Kennedy were interesting in that they formalized a great deal, yet also eased up a great deal. They were both accustomed to formal living and took to it naturally. On the other hand, their dancing, their gourmet dinners did much to take away the stiff overformality that had been associated with the White House.

In Washington, when "Honorable" is used in an address, it is always written in full and preceded by "The."

"Excellency" is not usually used when addressing American officials. It is used for a foreign president, cabinet officer, ambassador or high official or a former foreign high official.

A married woman does not share her husband's official title. The proper address is "The President and Mrs. Smith."

34

The United Nations

THE PRESENCE OF the United Nations in our country presents some special social and etiquette problems. Although this is true only to a degree in many sections, it is very much to the fore in New York City and adjacent communities.

The ambitious hostess who invites two or more U.N. delegates to dinner is faced with a dilemma when she starts to write her place cards. Who takes precedence? Is rank decided by country or by seniority in the U.N. Council? The U.N. Office of Protocol is always happy to solve the hostess' qualms. Actually there is a simple and sensible way of settling precedence.

Each year, just before the General Assembly, the names of all U.N. member nations are placed in a hat and the name drawn decides the ranking nation for that year. Thus, if Ireland is the name drawn, it outranks Italy and also Greece, Great Britain and all nations alphabetically before it, since for that year rank starts with "I."

This yearly information may be ascertained by watching for the press dispatch covering it in the newspapers about the time of the opening of the General Assembly. A hostess who entertains extensively and who "misses" the article in the papers may phone or write to the Office of Protocol of The United Nations to find out the ranking nation for the ensuing year. Naturally the hostess who suddenly finds herself faced with this precedence problem may do likewise.

Although there are, of course, some social functions, some socializing in the U.N., it is predominantly run on efficient, business-like (albeit diplomatic) lines. A newly arrived representative presents his credentials at once. Thereafter he or his wife may leave their visiting cards at the residence of their nation's consul, but this is decided by the diplomatic customs of their country; it is of no official concern to the United Nations.

There is, however, a special Hospitality Committee. The ladies on this committee are glad to help new arrivals with their problems. Obviously such a committee is of great assistance to the wife of a new representative and the wives of lesser personnel. Through the committee they can make social contacts and also obtain information about shops, city locations, customs in this country.

Since we are in a way hosts to the United Nations, it is not up to us to suggest that they wear Western attire or in other ways conform to our social customs. On the other hand, in a spirit of fairness it is not in the province of U.N. personnel to criticize American ways. While on U.N. property, they are *not* in our country and U.N. laws prevail; when they leave U.N. ground, they are in the United States and therefore they usually try to "fit into" the locality in which they reside. Thus courtesy demands that we treat them with the same consideration that we would accord any newcomer in our midst.

If U.N. personnel in general are a part of a community, take part in local school or church activities, they are accepted on their own value. The hostess who invites employees of the United Nations or those employed by nations in the U.N. has no problems about rank or precedence. In informal entertaining all guests in one's home are equal.

A representative is addressed as "Your Excellency" in U.N. matters. In his business and social contacts with us he may be addressed in this way or may be called "Mr. Jones" or "Prince John," depending on circumstances and how well we know him, and whether he has a title in his own country.

Below is the proper mailing form:

H. E.* Mr. John Dee
Permanent Representative of Iran to the U.N.
Permanent Mission of Iran
City Address

* H. E. is the abbreviation for "His Excellency."

35

Finally-

WHAT WE ARE aiming for is courtesy, graciousness and self-possession. If we worry over small details, we shall end by making others as uncomfortable as we are. "Did I word the introduction correctly?" "Should I have removed my glove?" "When is it permissible to leave this reception?" Everyone has found himself at some time in a ticklish or troublesome situation when he just wasn't quite sure of what to do. It is not possible to cover all these small perplexities in the regular chapters of an etiquette book, but perhaps by discussing some of the most frequently encountered problems in a question and answer form I can help others avoid embarrassing, often costly mistakes. Such is the purpose and hope of this chapter.

When personal and professional life merges . . .

I'd like to give my husband a photograph of myself for his office. Shall I autograph it?

No. A celebrity of screen or stage—in fact, anyone who is in the public eye—may autograph a picture on request. Others, however, should not do so. This is *especially* true for a photograph that is to be shown in your husband's office.

The executive vice-president's wife is in the hospital. Should I send flowers on behalf of my husband and myself?

If you have not met the woman, your husband should send the flowers or a card himself. If you know her, but not intimately, a book or card with a personal note may be appreciated even more than flowers. If you know her well and she is able to receive visitors, you will probably want to find out the hospital's visiting hours and pay a call in person.

A dinner is being given for my husband to honor his professional achievements. I know a toast will be proposed by the chairman. How should we respond?

Usually when a toast is offered the gentlemen present stand while the ladies remain seated and join in by lifting their glasses. If a "standing toast" is requested or a lady is toasted, the ladies rise. When the toast is proposed, your husband should remain in his seat but should not lift his own glass. After the others (including you) have drunk to the toast, he should rise and thank them briefly. If asked to, he may say a few words in response to the honor.

My account supervisor's wife has been thoughtful enough to invite our weekend guest to her dinner party on Saturday. As our guest will not know anyone at the party, including the host and hostess, should we help out by introducing him around ourselves?

Your desire to be helpful may be misinterpreted by your hostess. Don't take the chance. Properly speaking, you should present your friend to the hostess when you arrive at the party. She should then perform all the other necessary introductions. You can help her by enunciating your friend's name clearly when you introduce him to her.

The gentleman for whom I work as a secretary has invited me to a restaurant where there is a variation in price. Should I feel free to order whatever I like?

Presumably a man will not invite you to dine at a restaurant he cannot afford. However, if your compassion causes you continued discomfort, remember that it is always acceptable (and can be quite flattering!) to ask your escort to order for you, especially if he has selected the restaurant and eaten there before. You may assume he is able to make recommendations with authority—and this keeps the check under his control.

We were invited to a large open house given by my husband's regional manager. As we entered, another couple was leaving. The hostess spoke to us, then spoke to them, but did not introduce us to them. My husband says no snub was intended, but I feel slighted. Wasn't our hostess impolite?

No, she was not. A newly arrived visitor is never introduced to those who are taking leave. Let's hope, for your husband's sake, that your sense of injury did not show!

The chief surgeon in the hospital where my husband is on staff recently invited us to his country house for a weekend. I was much astonished by the note of invitation from our hostess—she not only told us what train we were to take on Friday afternoon, but also mentioned the train she expected us to leave by on Sunday night. This seems very rude, but I learned that the other weekend guests had been treated the same way. Is there any excuse for it?

It is quite customary and not at all rude. It has long been done by the English and is coming into use here more and more because it enables everybody—host and guests alike— to make definite plans. In fact, her treatment of people who live on doctors' schedules seems unusually considerate!

What can I do about people who, after they say "Goodbye" and start toward the door, keep on talking and starting new topics—and just never seem to be able to reach the point of going through the door? It drives me wild! Would it be too obvious to point out that tomorrow is a working day?

I'm afraid it would be considered impolite. Annoying as that kind of guests can be, you are really helpless about getting them out the door—unless you want to walk directly to it and open it yourself! If you can work the conversation around to the subject of your job or your husband's, your visitors *may* get the idea. But probably not. Wouldn't it be better to invite such guests only when you know you can sleep late the next day?

My husband is responsible for entertaining the branch office's vice-president when he and his wife are in town. As they are out-of-towners, it's possible they'd like to eat at a special restaurant or see a special show when they're here. Should we ask them what they want to do? Or should we plan the evening for them?

The v.p. and his wife will certainly not take offense if you make plans for their entertainment without consulting them, whereas you may embarrass them if you ask them to suggest the plans. Perhaps they will say they are longing to see a play to which you simply cannot get tickets, or they may feel embarrassed to define the expensiveness of the restaurant where you dine. If you have met them and have a casual friendship with them, it should be possible to ask their preferences without these difficulties. If not, however, you should know the resources of your own city well enough to plan an evening they are likely to enjoy.

A "lateral shift" was recently made in my husband's company and he feels a little bit injured. It is almost impossible not to have feelings of resentment about the individual who now has my husband's old job. This man will be present at a company function we are obliged to attend. Must we converse with him?

A polite guest owes it to his or her hostess never obviously to avoid speaking to another guest. This is true under any circumstances, even those as touchy as yours. You need not go out of your way to converse with the new man, but you do owe it to your hostess—and yourselves—to be courteous.

Should my husband's name be first on the signature of our Christmas card to office friends? I put my name first, but he says that this was wrong.

You were right. Your holiday cards, both business and personal, should be signed "Joan and David Green" if the signature is printed or engraved. When hand signed, this form is correct but it is also permissible for the actual signer to put the other's name first.

We have invited my husband's boss and his wife to dinner. How elaborate should our preparations be? Will they think we are apple-polishing if we "put on the dog?" Will they think we're neglecting them if we don't?

You should treat any guest as you assume he would want to be treated in his own home. In the case of your boss, assume the best about his home! You should offer the "best" to him of the food and service available within your *own* home. You needn't borrow finery to "put on the dog," though rental companies can now supply—for larger parties—an amazing variety of attractive tablewares when your own are not appropriate or you need a larger quantity. Make every effort reasonably to be expected from a person of your position and resources—but be sure the effort doesn't show.

In writing a letter to my doctor, whom I have known for several years, should I say "Dear Dr. Jones" or just "Dr. Jones?"

Write "Dear Doctor Jones;" and the word "doctor'" should not be abbreviated. Just "Dr. Jones" would be very abrupt.

What about office Christmas presents? Should someone in a subordinate position give presents to his superiors? Conversely, should a man give a present to his secretary?

Office Christmas presents are almost entirely a matter of custom in the particular office concerned. It is almost impossible to prescribe the correct thing in this matter. When you are not sure of the customs in your office (and you can find out quite a bit about this kind of thing around the water cooler), you should probably consider giving gifts only to intimate co-workers with whom you are good friends. It is always easier to accept a warm and grateful "thank you" than a gift you have not thought to reciprocate. A man can always show appreciation for someone who works under him by a small, thoughtful present. A modest gift from her boss ought not to embarrass a secretary who has not bought anything for him. Business girls can always offer homemade Christmas cookies to everyone in the office, or make some similar gesture, if they'd like to be festive at holiday time.

A member of my boss's family has died. Should I write a note of condolence myself, or should my wife do it?

Normally social correspondence is the duty of the wife, and your wife would write the letter from you both even though the person to whom sympathy is expressed is better known to you. If, however, your wife does not know the man, write your own letter. You may wish, if your boss is out of the office for a time, to write a note of your own *in addition* to your wife's. If so, be sure to use your personal (preferably white) stationery. Any personal note, however brief, is preferable to the printed "sympathy" card.

Is it proper for a man to address his wife as "Mrs. ———
———?" Should he speak of her as "Mrs. ——— ———?"
On what occasions?

Never address your wife as "Mrs. ——— ———." You
introduce your wife and speak of your wife to your employees as "Mrs. ——— ———." You introduce her and
speak of her to your social acquaintances as "my wife"—
never as "the wife" or "the little woman" or "the Missus!"
When speaking to friends, you refer to her by her first name.

Should water glasses be filled before my guests take their
places at the table?

Yes.

When business acquaintances took us to the theater we
were unlucky enough to arrive late. I noticed that the other
man's wife did not excuse herself as we took our seats. Is
this permissible? Is it considered distracting to speak as one
enters a theater late?

What could be more distracting than the annoyance of
someone who does not apologize for disturbing you? One
should be careful not to arrive late in the first place, but if
this can't be helped, wait for a suitable pause in the program or play and excuse yourself in a whisper as you go to
your seat.

For Smokers . . .

Is it ever correct for a woman to light another person's cigarette?

It is polite and respectful for a younger woman to offer to light the cigarette of an older woman. But she should be sure this gesture communicates her respectful attitude, and is not interpreted as a tactless reminder of the other woman's advanced years! A woman entertaining in her own home is merely being a thoughtful and attentive hostess when she offers the table lighter to a male guest who may not have seen it.

In a day and age when some of our most fashionable hostesses think nothing of smoking Danish cigars, is it ridiculously old-fashioned to ask a lady's permission to smoke?

If the women with whom you are talking are smoking, you hardly need to ask permission. If, however, no one else in the group is smoking, you merely preserve your good manners by asking, "Do you mind if I smoke?" Be especially careful about this if you plan to light up a cigar or pipe or a strong cigarette such as a Gauloise.

Should a woman ever ask permission to smoke?

When she visits the office or home of another woman, a lady who smokes should look for an ash tray. If none is provided, she does not ask permission to smoke (unless she is with an intimate friend). If there is an ash tray, however, she asks if she may light a cigarette.

I know I shouldn't talk with a cigarette in my mouth, but what about telephone conversations? Sometimes it's difficult to hold the phone, a pencil and a cigarette in your hands at the same time.

Put out your cigarette if you have to take extended notes on your call. It is unattractive to leave a cigarette resting in your mouth (you shouldn't get in the habit, even when no one can see you) and unintelligible to speak with one there.

What about guests who crush out their cigarettes on dessert plates or saucers? So many otherwise well-bred people do this.

If your guests smoke at dinner, ash trays should be conveniently placed at the table. If an ash tray is in front of a guest and he uses a dessert plate, drop him from your list!

On weddings . . .

My husband and I have been invited to the wedding of the daughter of one of the partners in my husband's law firm. We'd like to send a gift but have never met the bride and do not know her taste or needs. We feel in this particular situation it is very important not to seem to impose our own preferences and ideas. What should we do?

It's perfectly acceptable for you to telephone the partner's wife and ask at what department store her daughter has registered. The store's bridal consultant can then suggest a gift the bride has chosen at whatever price level you decide upon. The consultant can tell you the patterns of silver, china and glassware and chosen colors and designs in linens.

I am giving a bachelor dinner and my fiancée suggests that I give my ushers and the best man their gifts at that time. I say the gifts should be sent directly to the men's homes. Who is right?

Your fiancée is right about this. The gifts should be placed at the ushers' places at the dinner. Your gift to the best man should be at his place and may be the same or slightly handsomer. Bridesmaids' gifts are presented at the rehearsal dinner—never mailed—as they often consist of small articles of jewelry the bridesmaids will wish to wear in the wedding.

I am a divorcée and am about to remarry. My fiancé has never been married before. May I wear white and have a large wedding?

It is not appropriate to wear white or a veil for your second marriage. A simple but elegant afternoon dress and a hat would be in good taste. Only intimate friends and, of course, members of the family are invited to a second wedding, although a large party may be given for your engagement or after your return from the wedding trip to introduce your fiancé's friends to yours.

I am to be a bridesmaid for my cousin who lives out of town. I do not know her local friends. I have been told that on the day of the wedding the usher who will escort me during the ceremony calls for me at my hotel and gives me my bouquet. May I rely on this?

The usher neither calls for you nor escorts you during the ceremony. You go to the bride's home (in a taxi from your hotel, if necessary) and leave for the church from there. The bridesmaids' bouquets are supplied by the bride's family.

My fiancée and I have not announced our engagement, but our relatives and friends know we intend to very soon. Her cousin is being married shortly and I have not been invited. Should she go when I am not escorting her?

If only the immediate families of the bride and bridegroom are invited to the wedding you should not expect to be asked. If it is a larger wedding, your fiancée might casually mention the fact that you did not receive an invitation. It is quite possible that you were overlooked accidentally.

When people receive only an invitation to the church, should they go home after the wedding or stop at the bride's home and congratulate her parents?

Those who receive only an invitation to the church ceremony should go their way after the marriage is performed. It would be wrong to go uninvited to the bride's home.

An acquaintance of mine is about to be married for the second time. I haven't seen much of her since the death of her first husband, whom I knew well. Should I send a gift?

Relatives and intimate friends send gifts for a second marriage. Since you were better acquainted with the husband than with the woman herself, I really don't think a gift is necessary.

A girl I know quite well is marrying a man I know only slightly. Should I send a telegram of congratulation to her, using her maiden name, or to them both as "Mr. and Mrs. ———?"

The telegram should be delivered after the ceremony and should be addressed to "Mr. and Mrs. ———."

We are planning a small church wedding. Is it all right for the bridegroom to have his brother, who is divorced, act as best man?

If there is no law in your church regarding this there is no reason why the brother should not be best man. The clergyman who is to perform the ceremony can tell you if the church forbids it.

Concerning the telephone . . .

I must telephone the wife of my husband's department chairman to invite them to a party. How shall I refer to myself on the phone? I'm afraid she may not recognize me immediately.

You introduce yourself as "Alice Ingersoll"—not as "Mrs. Don Ingersoll," "Mrs. Ingersoll," "Don Ingersoll's wife" or "Mr. Ingersoll's wife." You can provide the chairman's wife with all the clues to which she is entitled by saying, "Don and I would be delighted if you and Professor Levine can join us on the seventh . . ." When you use her husband's professional title—and you should help her identify you by doing so—be sure that you use the correct one. For example, by courtesy an assistant professor is addressed as "Professor" rather than "Mister."

May I telephone my husband at the office when personal matters require it?

Personal or social calls at the office are distracting, time-consuming and can be very embarrassing to the person who receives them. The Chairman of the Board may be standing before your husband's desk when you call asking where the car keys are! Almost every company has an implicit or explicit policy against such calls during office hours, so don't leave your husband open to criticism. Remember that it is seldom as important as it may first seem to make that call *at that time*. Of course, there are exceptions and no one will blame you for calling when it is necessary. It's unfair to make extended social calls to anyone at an office, no matter how well-intentioned you may be. *You* may have ample leisure for social conversation during the day, but a working person's time is not his own. Be considerate.

My husband finds fault with me for making visits over the telephone. I don't see anything wrong in it—after all, I'm paying for the call, and why shouldn't I talk with my friends for as long as I like?

Your husband is right. It isn't only a matter of who pays for the call: it's a matter of considerateness. Your friend at the other end of the line may be too busy to take half an hour for trivialities with you and too polite to say so. Your long telephone call may prevent others from reaching her on more important business. A friendly brevity is desirable in telephone communications.

When the telephone is answered by someone other than the person you are calling, what is the proper thing to say?

You say "May I speak with Mr. Bryson, please?" or "I'd like to speak to Mr. Bryson, please." You may add, "This is Miss Larssen calling," or, if speaking to someone of your own or superior social position, "This is Karen Larssen calling." Identifying yourself will be appreciated as a courtesy and convenience to the person you are calling, especially if the telephone is answered by a switchboard operator or receptionist.

About the woman at the office . . .

My husband died three years ago. I still wear my wedding ring. Many of my friends say I should leave it off during business hours. Should I?

If you are known as a widow in the office there is no reason why you should not wear your wedding ring. A widow usually only removes her ring if she's about to be remarried.

My husband and I have been invited to have cocktails and dinner with his boss and the boss's wife. I'll have to go to their apartment directly from work to avoid being late. I know the boss's wife doesn't work and will be dressed for the evening. How can I avoid giving them the impression my husband is married to a frump, without being over-dressed all day?

Working women all over the country will sympathize with this basic problem, in whatever form it presents itself. I wish you luck in that often absurdly difficult process of shopping for a dress that is suitable for both daytime and evening wear in your particular area. In a large city, a conservatively cut dark silk suit might do the job. Or you might wear a scarf in the neck of a lower-cut dress during the day and remove it before you set out for the boss's apartment. You can probably carry a change of jewelry and evening make-up with you in your purse and freshen up at the end of the business day. Whatever compromise you reach, *don't* go home to change and be late for the party. And you have that valuable old truism on your side about its being better to be underdressed than over.

There are so many occasions when a working woman must decide on how much to leave for a tip . . . Could you give an easy rule about this?

Tipping is, as everyone who has tried it knows, a very complicated subject. Many women seem so paralyzed by nervous panic when it comes time to tip that they lose whatever mathematical powers they may once have had to translate percentages into specific figures, so as a blanket rule we might suggest taking 10 per cent and doubling that amount. Fifteen per cent to 20 per cent of the check is usually considered generous. Because tipping percentages vary from place to place, as do the kinds of service for which one is expected to tip, it is impossible to be more precise. If it is possible, a woman in a new city should make discreet inquiries. (For example, a woman from a small town in the Midwest who inquires at a New York beauty salon about tipping rates will be very surprised at the comparison with her local rate.)

Our office manager has made a rule that no one may powder or use lipstick at her desk. Do you think this is reasonable?

I think the office manager has a point. Even though it may be quite all right for a woman with a private office to make-up at her desk, unless there is a uniform ruling sooner or later girls will be applying mascara at the reception desk. And though gradually more and more cosmetic repair is becoming acceptable in public, a full-scale job is still most unappealing to watch.

I was a little disconcerted the other day when one of my publishing company's Spanish-born writers kissed my hand in the office in greeting me! Should I permit such things?

It is customary for a foreigner to lift the hand of a *married* woman to his lips in greeting. The hand of a young, single girl should not be kissed.

Although I have been working for several years and will continue in my present job after I am married, I do not wish to use a professional name. Will I confuse people if I do not keep my maiden name for work? How do I inform colleagues not invited to my wedding that I am no longer Miss Helen Black?

Unless you are so well-known in your profession by your maiden name that a very large number of people would be involved, you are perfectly free to change to your married name. People with whom you deal frequently can be informed of this quite casually on the telephone, and they should not construe such an announcement as a "hint" for a gift. It will assist those with whom you deal less frequently if for some time you sign your name as "Helen Black Johnston," rather than "Helen Johnston." Using your full name will identify you for them while at the same time they will notice that you have married. Your business signature, incidentally, should be typed

Helen Black Johnston
(Mrs. Frederick Johnston)

so that your colleagues will know how to address their letters to you. Though your full name should appear in the typed signature, you may sign yourself as "Helen Johnston," "Helen Black Johnston," "Helen," "Muffie" or whatever you like, depending on your relationship with the person you are addressing.

Index

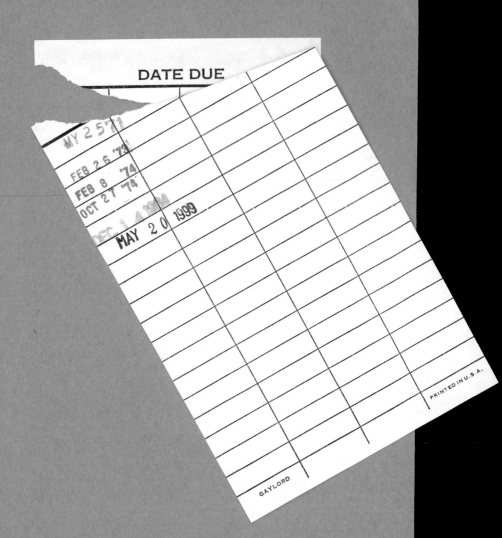